C H A P T E R   1

The Rise and Fall of the
Left Behind Series

The terms apocalypse *and* apocalyptic *have become standard parts of the vocabulary of modern society. Politicians warn of a nuclear apocalypse. Ecologists describe the apocalyptic effects of pollution, acid rain, and abuse of the environment.* Apocalypse Now *was the title of a movie that depicted the chaos and insanity of the Vietnam War. So commonplace have the terms become that when strong winds fanned a brush fire into a raging inferno in a Los Angeles suburb, one observer described the scene as "just like hell, like an apocalypse." Although apocalyptic terminology has become widely used, most people are unfamiliar with the literature from which the terms and the ideas originated. The best way to understand the meaning of apocalyptic terms, ideas, and motifs is to study apocalyptic literature itself.*

—*Apocalyptic Literature: A Reader*
Mitchell G. Reddish, editor

Why spend time reading, writing about, and critiquing a self-proclaimed fiction series about the end times? After all, it is fiction; it is make believe, right? Actually, there are numerous claims to the contrary. Dr. John Walvoord, former president of Dallas Theological Seminary, says of the first volume in the series, "The main features of this story are not fiction." Charles C. Ryrie,

1

editor of the *Ryrie Study Bible*, says, "Many scenes in this book could easily be the lead stories in tomorrow's news."[1] One of the authors of the series, Jerry Jenkins, claims, "These books are really about persuading unbelievers and encouraging believers with the story of what is going to happen in the end time, based on our interpretation of Bible prophecy."[2] In addition, the authorial team has written a companion volume titled *Are We Living in the End Times? Current Events Foretold in Scripture . . . and What They Mean.* Their two stated purposes for writing the book are: "1. To provide a basic companion outline of the end-time events and scriptural verification of the personages fictionalized in the Left Behind series; and 2. To show that we have more reason than any generation before us to believe Christ may return in our generation."[3]

These are but a few examples of the statements made by the authors of the Left Behind series and other "prophecy teachers" about the "truth" that is found in the series. While the series is fiction, it is based, according to the authors, on an accurate interpretation of Bible prophecy. The fiction series is filled with interpretations of biblical texts presented in lecture style by various fictional characters in the novels. Through the numerous speeches of these characters, LaHaye and Jenkins claim to present the correct interpretation of biblical prophecy and its application to current events. This book is an attempt to unearth the theological underpinnings of the Left Behind series and to challenge that claim, while providing an alternative means of understanding the biblical books of Daniel and Revelation.

This process begins in this chapter with an overview of the fiction series, its history, and its popularity. Chapter 2 describes and defines the theological framework, namely, premillennial dispensationalism, that provides the structure from which LaHaye and Jenkins interpret the Bible. This is followed by a discussion in chapter 3 of the sociopolitical ideologies that surface in the Left Behind series, with a special focus on how these ideologies evidence the

"The key to this [correct] theology is
non participation in evil." (146 + passim).

LEFT BEHIND?

THE FACTS BEHIND
THE FICTION

LeAnn Snow Flesher

99
"Critique"
137

Personal
reasons —
pp 139-40
(also "why?" —
126)
Critique Sum-
144.
"True" Gospel
Message - 149

JUDSON PRESS
PUBLISHERS SINCE 1824
VALLEY FORGE

LEFT BEHIND? The Facts behind the Fiction
© 2006 by Judson Press, Valley Forge, PA 19482-0851
All rights reserved.

Judson Press has made every effort to trace the ownership of all quotes. In the event of a question arising from the use of a quote, we regret any error made and will be pleased to make the necessary correction in future printings and editions of this book.

Unless otherwise indicated, Bible quotations in this volume are from the New Revised Standard Version of the Bible, copyright 1989, Division of Christian Education of the National Council of the Churches of Christ in the United States of America. Used by permission. All rights reserved.

Scripture quotations marked KJV are from the King James Version of the Bible.

Scripture quotations marked NIV are from the HOLY BIBLE, NEW INTERNA-TIONAL VERSION®. NIV®. Copyright © 1973, 1978, 1984 by International Bible Society. Used by permission of Zondervan. All rights reserved.

Library of Congress Cataloging-in-Publication Data
Flesher, LeAnn Snow.
Left behind? : the facts behind the fiction / LeAnn Snow Flesher.
    p. cm.
Includes bibliographical references.
ISBN 0-8170-1490-X (pbk. : alk. paper)
1. Millennialism. 2. Millennium (Eschatology) 3. Rapture (Christian eschatology) 4. Dispensationalism. 5. Bible—Criticism, interpretation, etc. 6. LaHaye, Tim F. Left behind series. I. Title.
BT892.F5 2006
236'.9--dc22   2006011620

Printed in the U.S.A.

13 12 11 10 09 08 07 06
10 9 8 7 6 5 4 3 2 1

CONTENTS

Why? See p. 126

sociocultural agenda of premillennial dispensationalism, which is, in turn, reinforced by the Left Behind narratives.

Chapter 4, titled "The Battle for the Bible," gives an overview of my own method of biblical interpretation set in contrast to the methods used by LaHaye and Jenkins. This discussion serves to prepare readers for the final section of the chapter, which offers working definitions of "prophecy" and "apocalypse," the two distinctive types of biblical literature that are most foundational to the end-times scenario presented by LaHaye and Jenkins. This is followed by traditionally accepted approaches to the interpretation of the books of Daniel and Revelation in chapter 5.

Two crucial doctrines for the belief system of LaHaye and Jenkins, and for the story line of their fiction series, are "the rapture" and "the tribulation." Chapters 6 and 7 offer a review and an analysis of their approach to the Bible as it is played out in developing these two doctrines. In addition, chapter 6 presents an overview and analysis of other pretribulational events, and chapter 7 gives an analysis of LaHaye and Jenkins's interpretation of Revelation as presented in the Left Behind series. A brief concluding chapter looks at the implications of LaHaye and Jenkins's interpretation for a contemporary world and offers insights for challenging this increasingly popular understanding.

Some familiarity with the novels and story line of the Left Behind series is necessary to follow the arguments of this book, so let's begin with a brief overview.

The Books and the Story

As of the writing of this book, fourteen novels have been published by Tim LaHaye and Jerry Jenkins: twelve in the original Left Behind series and two in a prequel series titled Countdown to the Rapture, for which a third book is scheduled to be released in June 2006. The table on page 5 outlines the titles of the Left Behind novels and the main events of the story they tell. The initial series begins with the rapture, after which those left behind spend much time piecing together what has happened and forming an anti-Antichrist militia force called the Tribulation Force. Meanwhile, the Antichrist, known only to those on the Tribulation Force as such, rises to power through a series of manipulations to rule the world. As a result, the need to declare allegiance to a particular camp, good or evil, is imposed upon the entire world's population. Those who profess faith in Christ are sealed with the mark of a cross on their foreheads, visible only to fellow believers.

In the meantime, the world has been suffering through the judgments outlined in the book of Revelation—first the seal judgments (chap. 6), then the first four trumpet judgments (8:1-12). At the sound of the fifth trumpet (9:1), a plague of scorpion-like locusts led by Apollyon, the chief demon of the abyss, is so horrifying that people try to commit suicide, but no one is allowed to die. As the Antichrist grows in power, one of the leaders of the Tribulation Force makes plans for his assassination at a global gala. Although his plan is bumbled, the Antichrist is assassinated by another person in the crowd. On the third day, at the funeral, the Antichrist rises from the dead, indwelt by Satan.

Now, at the midpoint of the seven-year tribulation, and as the embodiment of Satan, the Antichrist demands loyalty from all the earth's inhabitants, evidenced by their taking his sign, the mark of the Beast. Those who refuse are immediately publicly put to death by means of specially made guillotines that have been erected in public squares around the world. Now believers must go underground or take the mark of the Beast. In Jerusalem the Antichrist makes and fulfills his plans to desecrate the city and its Jewish temple and declares himself god. Meanwhile, a million threatened Jewish believers are transported to safety at Petra, an ancient Jordanian city. Things are heating up, and the Antichrist gathers troops from around the world at Megiddo in preparation for the

The Rise and Fall

Series Number	Novel Title	Date of Publication	Story Line
Prequel: Countdown to the Rapture			
1	*The Rising*	2005	The birth of the Antichrist
2	*The Regime*	2005	The Antichrist's initial rise to fame
3	*The Rapture*	2006	Countdown to the rapture
Initial Series: Left Behind			
1	*Left Behind*	1995	Making sense of the rapture
2	*Tribulation Force*	1996	Formation of the anti-Antichrist militia
3	*Nicolae*	1997	The Antichrist dominates the world
4	*Soul Harvest*	1998	Forced to choose between good and evil
5	*Apollyon*	1999	Release of the chief demon
6	*Assassins*	1999	Assignment: Jerusalem; Target: Antichrist
7	*The Indwelling*	2000	Satan takes possession of the Antichrist
8	*The Mark*	2000	The mark of the Beast forced on the world
9	*Desecration*	2001	The Antichrist proclaimed divine
10	*The Remnant*	2002	A million amassed at Petra as Armageddon nears
11	*Armageddon*	2003	The world prepares for the cosmic battle of the ages
12	*Glorious Appearing*	2004	The end of days; looking toward the millennium

cosmic battle of the ages. As the armies march against Petra and Jerusalem, Jesus appears in the sky riding on a white horse. At the sound of his voice, thousands of the Antichrist's soldiers fall down dead. Having defeated the Antichrist's armies, Jesus gathers all the people to the Valley of Jehoshaphat, where the sheep and the goats are judged in preparation for the millennium.

The History of the Series

The Rising, the title of the first volume of the prequel to the original Left Behind series, could be used to describe the entire series, as these novels have contributed to the rise of "prophecy belief" in the United States. ("Prophecy belief" refers to the perspective that as much as one-third of the Bible is prediction; much of which was fulfilled with the first coming of Jesus and the remainder of which will be fulfilled by Jesus' return.) Or have they? According to the authors, sales jumped following the events of September 11, 2001, because "millions of people suddenly [post-9/11] became interested in prophecy, hoping God had some answers to the unsettled and fearsome future that exists in our world. Whenever world tragedy hits, people look to the Bible for answers."[4]

Readers will indeed get answers in the fifteen-volume fiction series, but the critical question is, what is the basis for those answers? That question will be revisited later in this chapter and addressed in detail in the following chapters, but for now it will be helpful to begin with a look at the cultural phenomenon that is the Left Behind series.

With the first volume of the Left Behind series having been published in 1995, the authors and publishing house have already celebrated the tenth anniversary of the series with a classic collector's edition with special features added. And that's not all. A number of related products are being marketed, such as Left Behind: The Kids series, The Military series, The Political series, devotional books, calendars, abridged audio products, dramatic audio products, graphic novels (collections of comic books), and gift books and movies of the first three novels. It seems Tyndale House and authors Tim LaHaye and Jerry Jenkins hit a nerve. What has made this series so popular that individuals would want to purchase a special collector's edition or related merchandise?

While the first volume received modest attention and interest grew from 1995 to 2000 with the publication of each new novel, it was not until the catastrophic events of September 11, 2001, that interest in the series seemingly exploded. Volume 9, *Desecration*, published in 2001, was the first of the series to rise to number one on the *New York Times* list for best-selling fiction. Since then, three more volumes have been published to finish out the initial series, which was originally intended for seven volumes total, and the authors started a second, prequel, series. Currently, more than sixty million books have been sold. Left Behind has become a phenomenon!

From this brief sketch of the rise of the Left Behind series, we might draw two significant conclusions about its popularity: first, prophecy belief is far more central in American thought than previously recognized; and second, the explosion of interest in the series can be directly connected to the catastrophic events of 9/11. From these conclusions, we can further deduce that the American public has found within the Left Behind novels a means for interpreting and coping with the terrorist attacks of September 2001. While the impact of 9/11 is certainly not the only reason people read these novels, it appears to be a significant one. Why, we might ask, would so many people turn to *fiction* for help with concerns of such import?

While LaHaye and Jenkins readily admit the series is fiction, they also claim the books are based on what they refer to as a literal interpretation of Bible prophecy.[5] The fact is that the Left Behind phenomenon has changed the face of religious publishing. In the past decade, the series has been the subject of front-page articles in *Time* and *Newsweek* and of lead articles in many major daily newspapers, including the *New York Times*. In addition, stories about the books and their authors have been featured on the *Today*

Show, *60 Minutes*, CNN, MSNBC, the Fox News Channel, *The Morning Show*, *Good Morning America*, and thousands of talk radio stations around the world. Through this publicity, the authors claim that "millions of people who have never seriously considered their need for God have been brought face-to-face with the concept of redemption through Jesus Christ. The success of the books has driven the opportunity for an unprecedented harvest of souls."[6] It is certainly true that it would be difficult to find a Protestant churchgoer in the United States who has not heard of the Left Behind books, but we still must ask who is actually reading the novels from cover to cover and following the series from beginning to end—and why they are doing so.

Who Is Reading the Series?

Amy Johnson Frykholm explored the question of who is reading the Left Behind books as part of her doctoral research. Her results were published in 2004 by Oxford University Press under the title *Rapture Culture: Left Behind in Evangelical America*. Frykholm spent three years interviewing readers and attending their churches, Bible studies, and Sunday school classes. In the end, she had conducted thirty-five individual three-hour interviews. She found that while reading the novels was an individual recreational activity, the majority of the readers read in communities that are tied together by a common belief system. The typical Left Behind reader has found conversation partners in at least one network of family, friends, church family, or coworkers. Most often the reading community is a church group where the novels are read, shared, and discussed on a regular basis. One interviewee even reported having lost interest in the series but having continued to read the books simply because the group continued to read and discuss each new volume.

Most of Frykholm's interviewees were people who shared an appreciation of the Left Behind series. These readers reported diverse responses to the books, however. Some found the story line to be quite convincing and viewed the novels as accurate interpretations of the biblical texts, especially the book of Revelation. One woman reported being torn between whether the books are "just fiction" or as authoritative as the Bible.[7] Others revealed an awareness that they were reading fiction that embellished the biblical story line, while still other readers argued against specific details of the story as it interpreted end-time events. A few dissenters were also interviewed, mostly people who read one or two volumes, either by chance or because they were encouraged to do so by family members. This group, for the most part, found the books to be uninteresting and even annoying. One woman, whose daughter gave her volume one in hopes of bringing her to faith, said it was an interesting story but rejected its presentation of "God on a power trip."[8]

Those who favor the books often view them as tools for evangelism. In fact, the authors say that in addition to regularly receiving letters from readers who have had their relationships with Christ strengthened, they have received letters from people who have come to Christ as a result of reading the books.[9] While Frykholm heard several testimonies from readers that the books validated or strengthened their beliefs, she did not encounter any testimonies of people coming into a personal relationship with Jesus as a result of reading the books. Testimonies of how the Left Behind books assist readers in initiating conversations about the faith are not uncommon. The books seem to provide a nonthreatening venue for such conversation. Several readers have given volumes to "unsaved" family members and friends in hopes that the stories would bring them to faith in Christ. Others purposely read the books in public thinking that they were witnessing to their faith in Jesus as Savior by doing so. Yet those deemed "unsaved" who have received a Left Behind novel as a gift seldom found it to be meaningful in the way the giver had hoped.[10]

The preceding suggests, then, that the faithful readers of the Left Behind series are, for the most part, people who already share a common belief system among themselves and with the authors of the novels. It is interesting to note, however, that the interpretive communities of readers are not always in agreement. Even when read in the context of a shared belief system, the books lead to considerably varied responses. Thus, the series provides opportunities for dialogue and disagreement within communities of believers.

According to Frykholm's research, the range of responses by readers who appreciate the Left Behind series includes fear, hope, and a sense of elitism. For some, the return of Jesus and the end of history as presented in the series cultivates fear and doubt about their own salvation (or that of a loved one), coupled with fears of being left behind. Some of these readers reported feeling motivated to "get right with God" by getting their lives together, ending "unholy" or "ungodly" behaviors and turning toward doing the right and holy thing(s). For others the message of Left Behind provides hope for reconciliation and salvation, for tears turned to laughter and mourning into dancing. For many hope is found in the authors' suggestion that the rapture—the notion that believers will be snatched out of the world and taken to heaven—could take place within their own lifetime, allowing for escape from a world filled with pain and suffering without the experience of death.

Others read the rapture narrative primarily in terms of exclusion and elitism, finding within the novels secret privileged knowledge that only a select few can comprehend, thus reinforcing their idea that some will be left behind, and rightly so. One interviewee commented that, although he knows believers won't be given a choice, he would like to be left behind to serve as part of the special, secret resistance movement ("the Tribulation Force") that, in the novels, fights against the Antichrist.[11] For the majority of the committed readers, however, the content of the novels appeals to their conviction that the nonbeliever is the enemy. This ideological stance holds that the enemy is anyone who exhibits behavior that they deem to be antifamily, pro-feminist, pro-homosexual, pro-violence (not to be confused with a pro-war stance, as many Left Behind readers are pro-war but not pro-violence; note also that spokespersons from most conservative groups have spoken out in support of capital punishment and corporal punishment of children), and pro–global economy. Fundamentally, the rhetoric of the Left Behind series appeals to those who prefer to live in a simpler, less complicated world, where believers have a significant role due to the special knowledge they hold and where they can claim the credo "With God on our side, how can we lose?"

From a broader perspective, considering LaHaye's statement that people look to the Bible for answers whenever tragedy hits, it is clear that we do live in a world where humans are continually looking for a meaningful pattern within the chaotic events that surround us. LaHaye's claim has some validity, but it is limited in its focus. Indeed, it is true that in the throes of tragedy, people look for wisdom and meaning, but not everyone turns to the Bible. The past decades have in fact seen an explosion of alternative sources of comfort and explanation. These alternative sources include tales of near-death experiences, testimonies of UFO sightings and alien abductions, visions/appearances of the Virgin Mary, and the New Age Movement. The Left Behind series is but one response, one offering of wisdom for tough times and hope in a world that has seemingly gone mad. What makes the Left Behind phenomenon stand out, however, is its overwhelming popularity, readily measured in the sales of books. And so we return to the key question of why this series is so popular.

The Challenge of Left Behind
One pastor's story can offer some insights on the popularity of this fiction series. Jason Byassee writes in his article "Enraptured: What's Behind 'Left Behind'?" that he had never met anyone who

believed in the rapture—not in college, not in seminary, not in his evangelical fellowship groups—until he received his first rural church assignment. At that time, he came to realize that he was the only person in the congregation who did not believe that true believers would be snatched away to heaven by the returning Christ: "My parishioners simply assume that this is what the Bible teaches. And why shouldn't they—they've never heard otherwise from their preachers."[12]

The members of Byassee's church were functioning with beliefs drawn from a theological system known as "dispensationalism," of which the rapture is a critical component. Premillennial dispensationalism is the version of this system that provides the theological grid through which the authors of the Left Behind series interpret Scripture and develop their novels. The authors' "literal interpretation" (a phrase that has come to be equated with "the only valid interpretation") is in fact guided by a system of belief that was developed in the mid-1800s by a man named J. N. Darby. This theological system is imposed on Scripture rather than allowing the biblical text to speak for itself.

We will examine the history and content of premillennial dispensationalism in detail in chapter 2; and in later chapters, we will explore how Bible texts are forced into service to support particular components of the belief system. For now, it is critical to make three key points: First, those who are reading and celebrating the Left Behind series are laypeople who believe in aspects of this theological system and find reinforcement for those beliefs in the novels. Pastors do not tend to read the novels; and even when their pastors clearly disapprove of the series, parishioners continue to read and share the books. Second, the majority of the Christian world does not hold to dispensationalism, premillennial or otherwise. Although the words *premillennial* and *dispensational* do pop up from time to time in theological discourse, few people, if any, truly understand the system to which one must adhere in full in order to agree with the interpretation of the end times as presented by LaHaye and Jenkins. For the most part, biblical scholars would be in serious disagreement with this belief system (and much of what LaHaye and Jenkins are purporting to be biblical truth); however, they generally do not even bother to engage it or the writings that flow from and perpetuate it. And third, similar to the experience reported by Byassee, most pastors do not know enough about dispensationalism to have an intelligent conversation about the topic.

The sad reality is that while this theological system and the social and political ideologies that are formed by it are growing in popularity and social and political influence, the majority of seminaries and pastors have ignored the phenomenon. The result is that pastors and seminary professors are interpreting and teaching the Bible from one set of understandings while the premillennial dispensational, self-designated "prophecy teachers" are teaching from a very different theological basis. Consequently, laypeople who engage teachings from both arenas are receiving mixed messages, from which they are building their own working theologies. In the end, faithful church attendees embrace a working theology that is inconsistent at best and dysfunctional at its worst. Seminary professors and pastors from a wide spectrum of theological stances, conservative to liberal, can no longer afford to ignore the phenomenon the premillennial dispensational prophecy teachers are sustaining.

The teachings on the end times (what scholars refer to as "eschatology") found in the Left Behind series are seriously problematic for several reasons. First, they perpetuate a massive misunderstanding of the nature of Scripture and how Scripture should be studied. Second, they create and support a separatist worldview in which all who disagree are deemed "the enemy." Finally, the mixed-up working theology of church members may thwart (and likely already has thwarted) healthy forward movement in local congregations. The implications of these outcomes can lead to some far-reaching, extremely serious, and even disastrous consequences. We have seen two very extreme examples of these consequences in our own lifetime in Waco, Texas, and San Diego, California.

The Waco Branch Davidian group began in 1929 under the name Davidians when Victor Houteff, a former Seventh-day Adventist, became convinced the church had compromised its commitment to holiness. After Houteff's death, he was succeeded by his wife, who lost credibility when her prediction of Christ's return in 1959 did not materialize. By then Ben Roden had established a new group called the Branch Davidians, built off the excitement of the founding of Israel in 1948 and the Six-Day War in 1967. This group managed to gain control of Mount Carmel. In 1987 Vernon Howell, who later changed his name to David Koresh, assumed control of the group. Through his marathon Bible studies in which he demonstrated how to systematize prophecy and his claims to unlock the seven seals of the scroll mentioned in Revelation 5, Koresh was able to win the group's loyalty. Due to his teaching that the kingdom would come only through violence and his stockpiling of weapons, federal agents took action against him and the community in 1993. In the end, eighty Branch Davidians, including Koresh, died in the fire that erupted during the federal assault.[13] In 1997 thirty-nine members of Heaven's Gate, a San Diego–based New Age millennialist movement under the leadership of Marshall Applewhite, committed suicide. The group believed—based on a combination of astrology, New Age philosophy, and Christian millennialism—that an immanent judgment was coming and sought to escape to a better place.[14]

It is high time for some education, teaching, and preaching on the topic of popular end-times theologies. For while the popularity of the Left Behind series will eventually come to an end, the teachings of premillennial dispensationalism will live on in the hearts and minds of the general population, awaiting another opportunity for exploitation.

CHAPTER 2

What Is Premillennial Dispensationalism?

Shortly after the publication in 1841 of my work "On the Second Coming of Our Lord before the Millennium," a brother in the ministry met me in the street. "I hear, Brother R.," said he, "that you have published a book on the premillennial coming of our Lord." I replied that I had, and that if he would call on me I would give him a copy of the work. He thanked me for the offer, but never came for the book. Just as we were about to separate he laid his hand on my shoulder, and in a very persuasive tone said, "My dear brother, do let me advise you to stop your studies of the prophecies. I never knew a man who began to study them and to write on them who did not ultimately go crazy."

—William Ramsey,
Messiah's Reign: The Future Blessedness of the Church and the World, 1857

Throughout history most Christians have believed in God's providential oversight of world events and of an end-time consummation. The study of the end of the world as we know it has been termed *eschatology*, which literally means the "study of last things." Two thousand years of Christian thinking has resulted in much debate and numerous conclusions about what the Bible says about the end times. This chapter provides a very brief overview of the predominant Christian eschatological beliefs held throughout the centuries and then locates the system of belief adhered to by the authors of the Left Behind series within that larger context.

Christian Understandings of Last Things

No doubt readers will have heard a variety of terms related to the study of the end times—terms such as *rapture, premillennial, post-millennial, amillennial, pretribulation, posttribulation, dispensation, apocalyptic, eschatological,* and many more. These terms frequently become confused and confusing, so we will begin with some basic definitions and a sense of the flow of thought from the early church to the fourth century and finally to the modern era.

It is important to note that of all of the theological categories that have been studied and debated throughout the ages, eschatology has received the least amount of attention in the big picture. While some groups, such as the premillennial dispensationalists, have focused the majority of their interpretive energies on the study of the last things, the majority of Christendom has not. In fact, most theological textbooks present eschatology at the end, as do most theological courses in the seminary. Consequently, the study of last things is most often held as "the last thing" to be studied. Frequently, this means the subject receives minimal attention by those being trained for the ministry. Nevertheless, eschatology is clearly an important theological category for the Christian church and, as such, deserves our full attention.

Millennial Views

The term *millennium* refers to the time period described in Revelation 20:5 when those martyred for the faith come to life and reign with Jesus for one thousand years. Literal readers, such as the *premillennialists*, believe this verse is saying that Jesus will return to earth and establish a literal physical kingdom over which he will reign as King for one thousand years. Premillennialists believe the world, and consequently humanity, will become increasingly more evil, violent, and faithless, as was the case in Noah's day. This path toward destruction will lead to a cataclysmic moment in which God will come supernaturally to judge evil, punish the wicked, and establish the kingdom of heaven on earth, over which Jesus will rule as King. This kingdom will include a time of great abundance and fertility, of renewing the earth and rebuilding a glorified Jerusalem. Fundamentally, premillennialism flows from a pessimistic view of the human potential for reform. While it is probably true, as many have supposed, that the early church looked to an imminent future return of Christ and an earthly millennial reign,[1] not all leading thinkers of the early church agreed with the emphasis on abundance for the believer.[2]

In the fourth century, premillennialism fell out of favor largely due to the influential theologian Augustine's teaching that the millennium does not lie in the future, but has already begun. In his famous work *City of God*, Augustine purported that the church was already living in the millennium, which began with Christ's first coming, and that the one thousand years was not to be taken literally. According to Augustine, the ministry of grace in the church was the realization of the eschatological hope.[3] Augustine was writing in response to the new status the church enjoyed following the conversion to Christianity of the Roman emperor Constantine in 312 CE. Given the new climate of tolerance for the Christian church, which eventually led to its status as the official religion of the empire, this postmillennial view became dominant.

Postmillennialists believe the preaching of the gospel of Jesus Christ will be so successful that the world will be converted, evil will be banished, and then Christ will return. In other words, the literal physical establishment of Christ's earthly kingdom will come as a result of a long cycle of human progress and moral advance achieved through the prayerful efforts of Christian believers. This optimistic view became the dominant view for evangelicals in the eighteenth and nineteenth centuries, claiming such luminaries as Jonathan Edwards and A. H. Strong.

A final group of millennialists, the *amillennialists*, may more accurately be named nonmillennialists. This group does not look for a literal thousand-year reign of Jesus on earth, but foresees a transcendent spiritual fulfillment of Christ's ultimate triumph that stands outside of time and space as we know it. Amillennialism is frequently confused with postmillennialism because they hold in common the view that the one-thousand-year reign is to be taken symbolically and that the millennium is in fact the church age. Where they differ is that the postmillennialist, unlike the amillennialist, believes Jesus will have an actual future earthly reign. It is possible that postmillennialism and amillennialism were not sharply distinguished in the first nineteen centuries. However, when postmillennialism fell out of favor in the twentieth century, amillennialism became the substitute. Amillennialism has enjoyed its greatest popularity in the period since World War I.

Tribulational Views
Also important for this conversation are the different understandings of a time of trial referred to as "the tribulation" and the presence (or nonpresence) of the church throughout that time. Those holding a *pretribulational* perspective believe the time of trial described in the book of Revelation will be a great tribulation that has been unparalleled in history and from which the true church will be snatched away (raptured) by Christ before it begins. In this view, Christ does not return one time, but two times. His first return is secret and known only by true believers. Those who are left behind will only know that a certain part of the population is missing. When Christ comes again a second time, every eye will see him in his glory, and there will be a judgment and millennial reign.

Posttribulationalists believe that Christ will not come for the church until the tribulation is over. Posttribulationalists avoid the use of the word *rapture*, and believe the church will be present on earth throughout the great tribulation but will be kept from it much the same way the people of Israel lived through the plagues brought upon Egypt in the book of Exodus but were not touched by them.

There are variations of these tribulational ideas, the most popular of which is the *midtribulational* perspective. In this view, the church will experience only the first half of the tribulation, which is understood to be less extreme. Then, just before the wrath of God is poured out in the bowl judgments (often termed the great tribulation, from Revelation 16–17), Jesus will return to remove the church from the earth.

Classifications of Interpretive Views
Also important for understanding the spectrum of eschatological belief is the stance from which a community (or individual) interprets the Bible—whether a faith community is futurist, historicist, preterist, or idealist. *Futurists* hold that most of the prophecies described in Scripture will come to pass in the future at the close of the age. Thus they read biblical prophecy as a prediction of events yet to come. For example, futurists believe that everything found in the book of Revelation after chapter 3 has not yet occurred, and they look to the future for its fulfillment.

Historicists believe that the events described in biblical prophecy were in the future at the time of the writing and refer to events that would take place throughout the history of the church. Consequently, historicists search the pages of history as well as current news headlines for events that have taken place in fulfillment of Scripture.

A true futurist will not equate current events with specific biblical prophecies, but will only acknowledge current events as *signs* of the coming of the end. In contrast, a historicist might equate today's headlines with a specific biblical prophecy. For example, the futurist interprets the recent development of the European World Market as a *sign* that the end is near, and a historicist may interpret the same event as a fulfillment of the prophecy of the ten horns on the terrifying fourth beast of Daniel 7:7.

Preterists believe that the events described in Daniel and Revelation were taking place at the time of the writer and thus are to be understood as past events. For example, preterists would understand the ten horns of the fourth beast described in Daniel 7:7 to represent the ten rulers who succeeded Alexander the Great.[4] And *idealists* believe that events described in Daniel and Revelation are to be understood as symbolic, not limited to a particular place and time, and as timeless truths. While the first three groups, the futurists, historicists, and preterists, would all agree that the ten horns of the fourth beast found in Daniel 7:7 represent kingdoms (albeit kingdoms with very different identifications), idealists would focus on the timeless truths the imagery is intended to teach. Much more will be said about the interpretation of Daniel's images as we proceed through this book.

Nineteenth- and Twentieth-Century Eschatologies

In the nineteenth century, evolutionary theory, scientific method, and critical study of the Bible were embraced and blended with religious thought, resulting in a "liberalized" understanding of last things. For this *modernized eschatology*, the kingdom of God came to be understood as the ethical rule of God in human hearts. Christians were called to spread this kingdom in the present, and the concept of the Second Coming was understood as the truth of the victory of God's righteousness over evil in the world,[5] which would be achieved through the Christianization of the social order.

As might be suspected, the religious world, both liberal and conservative, disapproved of these modern eschatological ideas. In response, Albert Schweitzer, a medical doctor and theologian, countered *demodernized eschatology*. He emphasized that Jesus did preach of a future kingdom that would be supernatural, would come through cosmic upheaval, and would be unlike anything humanity had experienced to date and that his teachings were incorrect. Instead, Jesus died a martyr's death and now reveals himself to those who obey his commands and perform his tasks.[6] Schweitzer concluded that the Jesus who has spiritually risen within the hearts of humans is the one who is significant for our time.[7]

Like Schweitzer, believers in *realized eschatology* held that eschatological teaching permeated the teachings of Jesus but insisted Jesus' message was not about a future kingdom. Instead, according to C. H. Dodd, who developed this view, the coming of Jesus was the coming of the kingdom of God, God has already triumphed, Satan has already fallen from heaven (Luke 10:18), judgment has already taken place (John 3:19), and the Christian already possesses eternal life (John 5:24).[8] This is a preterist position as outlined above—biblical prophecies have already been fulfilled.

Following on the heels of and in critique of realized eschatology, came a *proleptic* and an *inaugurated eschatology*. The term *proleptic* refers to treating a future event as if it has already happened. This view sees in the ministry of Jesus, in his death and resurrection, signs of the age to come, and also certain components of the kingdom of God that are still to be realized.[9] Adherents of this perspective frequently speak of a tension between the "already" and the "not yet"—that is, between the components of the kingdom of God that already exist through the life and ministry of Jesus and the Christian church, and the components of the kingdom that are yet to be realized.

The *social gospel*, made famous by Walter Rauschenbusch, taught that the real nature and purpose of Christianity must be found in the teachings of Jesus and in particular in his phrase "the reign of God." Jesus proposed a kingdom of God on earth, not in heaven, and accordingly, the kingdom of God was both future and present, and was understood as a social order in which "the worth and freedom of every least human being will be honoured and protected; in which the brotherhood of man will be expressed in the common possession of the economic resources of society; and in which the spiritual good of humanity will be set high above the private profit interests of all materialistic groups." Thus the kingdom of God is in the church and in all ethical and spiritual progress of humankind. There is no final societal consummation, but hope in a personal consummation.[10]

Dispensationalism arose in the mid-1800s and is viewed primarily as a system for interpreting Scripture. Dispensationalists find in the Bible evidence of a series of dispensations, or economies, under which God has ordered and managed the world. At the core is the conviction that Scripture is to be taken literally, which does not necessitate that all symbols be taken literally, but holds that if the plain meaning makes sense, then readers need look no further.[11] Therefore, passages about the second coming of Jesus are not only taken as literal, but the kingdom of heaven is seen to constitute the fulfillment of Scripture for the Jews, as a literal, physical kingdom with Jesus as monarch.

This overview of nineteenth- and twentieth-century eschatologies has been given to provide you with a sense of the breadth of thought that has come out of Christianity in modern times. The categories of millennialism, tribulationalism, and interpretive approaches are mutually exclusive. This means that any one individual (or group) can locate himself or herself in each major category. For example, someone could be a premillennial, pretribulational futurist or a postmillennial, pretribulational historicist, and so on. It all depends on how one understands the millennium, the tribulation, and the interpretation of Scriptures as depicted in the following chart.

Premillennial Dispensationalism

Eschatological (or End-times) Perspective	Millennial Views	Tribulational Views	Interpretive Views
Modernized Harnack	Amillennial	Nontribulational	Idealist
Demodernized Schweitzer	Amillennial	Nontribulational	Preterist and Idealist
Realized, Dodd	Amillennial	Nontribulational	Preterist
Proleptic Robinson	Amillennial	Nontribulational	Preterist and Futurist
Social Gospel Rauschenbusch	Amillennial	Nontribulational	Idealist
Dispensationalism	Premillennial	Pre-, Post- or Mid-tribulational	Futurist or Historicist
Left Behind	Premillennial	Pretribulational	Futurist

The understanding of last things, or the eschatological view, that drives the Left Behind series is premillennial, pretribulational, and futuristic. This means that the authors are teaching through the series that Jesus will return to earth at the close of a seven-year tribulation to establish a kingdom over which he will reign for a thousand years; Jesus will secretly come prior to the seven-year tribulation to gather his faithful ones and remove them from the earth; and most of the prophetic promises given in Scripture are still to be fulfilled in the future. LaHaye and Jenkins are a subgroup under the larger category of dispensationalism, which has a variety of versions. Some dispensationalists, for example, are post- or midtribulational; some fall under the category of historicist when it comes to the interpretation of Scripture.

As the chart above reveals, the modernized, demodernized, realized, proleptic, and social gospel eschatologies are all amillennial, which stands to reason after World War I. Before the First World War, many Christians were postmillennialist, but the negativity and brutality of the war stole away the optimistic view that the world was becoming Christianized and heading toward a literal millennial reign and replaced it with the nonmillennial perspective, which emphasizes the presence of the kingdom of God within the heart(s) of humans. Modern eschatologies that are not dispensational are also not tribulational. This makes sense since a symbolic understanding of the millennium suggests a symbolic understanding of tribulation. While these views hold that the church goes through tribulation by virtue of its existence as a community within a hostile larger culture, they do not expect a literal cataclysmic tribulation.

The modernized, demodernized, realized, proleptic, and social gospel perspectives also reveal a variety of approaches to interpreting the Bible. The chart portrays each group's primary commitments, although each most likely fits into more than one category. For example, the modernized, with its emphasis on ethics, falls under the category of idealist. For this group the majority of scriptural events described, especially those that are supernatural in nature, are understood to be metaphorical. The table on page 23 outlines a spectrum of eschatological thought in the modern age (i.e., the nineteenth and twentieth centuries). Since the authors of the Left Behind series fall under the broader category of premillennial dispensationalists, it will help to review where this system of belief came from.

The Historical Development of Premillennial Dispensationalism

Premillennial dispensationalism is a theological system with a primary emphasis on biblical interpretation developed by John Nelson Darby (whose "inspiration" came, in part, from the efforts of Edward Irving,) which was popularized (plagiarized) in the United States by Cyrus Ingerson Scofield.[12] John Nelson Darby was born of Irish parents in London in November 1800. He spent his early years in Ireland, where he gained his education. After graduation he entered the legal profession and was called to the Irish Chancery Bar in 1822. He abandoned this profession, however, one year later following a conversion experience. Though never theologically trained, Darby was ordained a deacon in the Church of England in 1825 and threw himself into the work of the church with great abandon. His efforts were met by such a tremendous spiritual awakening among those to whom he ministered that he was ordained a minister one year later.

While Darby was in Dublin for his ordination, the archbishop issued a decree that essentially demanded that all converts to the church swear allegiance to the king. Disillusioned by this decree, Darby left the Church of England in search of a body of believers who shared his view of sole allegiance to Christ. He quickly found a group who met together for mutual edification through prayer and Bible study. Under Darby's leadership, this group developed into the Brethren Movement, which eventually became known as the Plymouth Brethren. It was during this time, in part through a personal revelation about the distinct natures of Israel and the church, that Darby developed "dispensationalism." Though many Christians had used periodization as a way of understanding the history of God's revelation and relationship with people, Darby was the first to create a full-blown dispensational system of interpreting Scripture. The system was built from a doctrine of dispensations and covenants. According to Darby, history can be divided into seven dispensations. These dispensations are:

1. innocence (Genesis 1:28 to the expulsion from Eden),
2. conscience (Genesis 3:7 to the flood),
3. human government (Genesis 8:15 to the call of Abraham),
4. promise (Genesis 12:1 to the covenant at Mount Sinai),
5. law (Exodus 19:1 to the death of Christ),

6. grace (Pentecost, Acts 2:1 to Christ's Second Coming), and

7. kingdom (the Second Coming to the great white throne judgment).

These dispensations are built off of, but are not in every case directly related to, the various covenants that God has established with humanity throughout the ages.[13] Darby's system made its way across the Atlantic to spread into conservative evangelicalism in the 1870s during a preaching tour in which he won over several key evangelical leaders, including Cyrus Ingerson Scofield.

C. I. Scofield, born in Michigan in 1843 and raised in Tennessee, was a lawyer turned Bible teacher. He served the Confederate army during the Civil War, after which he moved to St. Louis, where he married and became an attorney. Scofield later moved, with his wife and family, to Kansas, where he served as a representative to the Kansas legislature and also worked as a U.S. attorney under the appointment of President Ulysses S. Grant. Scofield was forced to resign this office under accusations that he had stolen political contributions intended for Senator John Ingalls. Shortly thereafter his marriage fell apart, and he returned to St. Louis, where he eventually landed in jail for forgery.[14]

In 1879, while in jail, Scofield had a conversion experience that caused him to focus his life in entirely new directions. After his conversion, Scofield remarried and, under the mentorship of prominent pastor James H. Brookes, became deeply immersed in dispensationalism and evangelical activism. Three years after his conversion, Scofield, without any formal theological training, became pastor of a small Congregational church in Dallas, Texas. In 1888 Scofield published *Rightly Dividing the Word of Truth*, a popularized explanation of Darby's dispensational system. In 1890 he developed the Scofield correspondence course, and in 1902 he began work on the *Scofield Bible*. In 1909 Oxford University Press published *The Scofield Reference Bible*, which consisted of a set of chain references, headings, and a commentary, all prepared by Scofield himself, added to the King James Version of the Bible.

The Scofield Reference Bible became one of the most influential religious works of the twentieth century (in the U. S.). While the work was not used in seminaries for the most part, it was used widely in Bible schools, many of which had been established to teach dispensationalism. According to many, the *Scofield Bible* was so widely used in churches that in many circles it became the work to which Christians appealed to end all theological controversies. In fact, a few have suggested that laypeople who studied Scofield's Bible understood themselves to be illuminated beyond their own pastors.

The popularity of and commitment to *The Scofield Reference Bible* are due in part to two important factors. First, Scofield's interpretive commentary was placed on the pages of the King James Bible itself, so readers frequently confused Scofield's commentaries with biblical texts, not remembering which ideas came from which. As theologian Albertus Pieters noted in a 1938 lecture, "The confidence of the reader in writings divinely inspired is unconsciously transferred to and shared by the other remarks on the same page."[15] Given that the Bible was understood as the inerrant and infallible word of God, Scofield's interpretive comments, found on every page of the biblical text, gained the same reputation. Second, Scofield wrote his commentary with an authoritative attitude in which he never argued, explained, apologized, or provided reasons for his assertions of truth. The effect was to inspire tremendous confidence in readers that they were receiving "the truth"—so much so that Dr. T. T. Shields of Toronto is quoted as saying, "From a position of entire ignorance of the Scriptures to the position of oracular religious certainty—especially respecting eschatological matters—for some people requires from three to six months with the Scofield Bible."[16]

Recent historians have suggested the *Scofield Bible*'s popularity grew considerably during and immediately following World War I. Thus, much like the observed increased interest in the Left Behind series following 9/11 in the United States, public interest turned to the teachings found in the *Scofield Bible* during times of crisis.[17]

Key Features of Premillennial Dispensationalism

In addition to the seven dispensations mentioned above, Darby established and Scofield later popularized several key features of a very complex system of belief. Many of these features are outlined in the following section, as are logical deductions that arise from the system. It is important to note that not all premillennial dispensationalists agree on every point of the system. For the purpose of this project, I am striving to present the system as Darby and Scofield did, and to note how the Left Behind series either adheres to or deviates from the original presentation of the system.

The key features of the premillennial dispensational system include: a dichotomy between Israel and the church; a narrowly defined "true church" in contrast to the church; a rigidly applied literalism in the interpretation of the Bible; an understanding of the kingdom as a postponed, entirely future Jewish reality; a restricted view of the church; a rapture that precedes a seven-year tribulation; a second opportunity for Jews to receive Christ's kingdom; a distinction between law and grace; and the compartmentalization of Scripture.

The key to comprehending the system is the unique "revelation" Darby received while reading of the book of Ephesians—that Israel and the church are dichotomous entities, which is to say that any time Israel is mentioned in the Scriptures, it is taken to mean "ethnic Israel," or the literal people and nation of Israel, who are distinct from the Gentiles. In this system, the Gentiles are equated to the church, which is understood as the literal body of Christ, the habitation of God, while Israel is attached to the earthly kingdom. The "true church," however, does not include all Gentiles. Only

28

those who have kept themselves pure and holy through the power and presence of the Holy Spirit at work in their lives are members of the "true church." Thus the church and the "true church" are separate entities. Only the "true church" is the body of Christ and will thus become the bride of Christ in the end.

Of equal importance is the presupposition of a rigidly applied literalism in the interpretation of Bible prophecy. This means that every word of Scripture must be taken literally, and its meaning must not be spiritualized. This approach does not rule out symbolism, figures of speech, or typology, but insists that "the reality of the literal terms involved" determines meaning.[18] To this day, a nonliteral interpretation is equated with liberalizing tendencies and thus, according to the premillennial dispensationalist, denies the validity of the Word of God. Thus, the premillennial dispensationalist concludes that God has bound God's self to fulfill every promise to Israel exactly as it has been written. And Christ's future reign on earth, the millennial kingdom, will be for the purpose of fulfilling promises made to Israel that have not yet been fulfilled.

This literal, rigid reading of Scripture coupled with the idea of distinct dispensations leads to the conclusion that the nation of Israel, inclusive of ancient Israelites and contemporary Jews, is on one track and the Christian church on quite another. The result is that God's expectations for each group are very different as is God's treatment of each. Along this line, the system purports that Jesus originally came more than two thousand years ago to usher in a literal, physical, theocratic kingdom (the kingdom of heaven) but was rejected by the Jews, with the result that the kingdom was never established. Consequently, when Jesus comes again, he will establish the kingdom of heaven on earth, and that kingdom will be populated by Jews (144,000 Jewish evangelists and their converts) who survive the tribulation. The "true church," however, will be snatched away before the tribulation to reside in its rightful place in the heavens as Christ's bride. After the millennial reign, the saints of the "true church," who have been with God in heaven, will be transferred to the new Jerusalem (Revelation 21–22), where they will dwell with God, Jesus, the Holy Spirit, the redeemed of Israel, and the unfallen angels. The city will not be in heaven but will have a particular location.[19]

Also significant is the distinction between law and grace, the former being the basis for the "gospel of the kingdom" for Israel and the latter the basis for the "gospel of grace" for the church. While this assertion may be vigorously denied among dispensationalists, the logical conclusion of the distinctions between law and grace and Israel and the church, and of different relations of God to humans in the different dispensations is inevitably that humans are not saved the same way in all ages. Hence, Scripture is divided according to classes of people. No single passage of Scripture can have primary application to two dispensations at the same time. Only those passages specifically addressed to a child under grace are to be given primary application to the church, and conversely, those addressed to a child under law are to be given primary application to the Jewish population. Certain parts of the Bible are therefore restricted to certain people, and entire groups may be exempt from other parts.

By now most readers will have noted characteristics of premillennial dispensationalism with which they are familiar, with which they agree or have agreed at one time, or which they reject. Who among Protestants in the United States, for example, has not heard of the concept of the rapture? I remember as a child being taught about it in Sunday school, talking about it with my friends, and even engaging in "rapture practice," where we would calmly walk along the road and then catapult ourselves into the air, arms reaching heavenward. The rapture is a fascinating idea—especially considering the consequences of not being raptured. Yet it is important to recognize that this concept, as well as other components of the premillennial dispensational system, flows from a peculiar and intricate approach to understanding Scripture. In upcoming chapters, we will look more closely at some of the key beliefs of this complex system and review some of the elaborate biblical interpretive practices that are necessary to support them, but first let's take a moment to compare aspects of this perspective with classic Christian thought.

Premillennial Dispensationalism Compared with Historic Christianity

The preceding survey of Christian understandings of the end times reveals that the notions of a tribulation for the Jews and a rapture for true believers are recent and marginal beliefs within Christian eschatology. Additionally, while theologians have long struggled to understand and define God's self-revelation and relationship to people as it has developed throughout different periods of history, the idea of distinct dispensations in which people are tested in respect of obedience to some specific revelation of the will of God[20] runs contrary to the basic Christian understanding that God is the same yesterday, today, and forever. Historically, the Christian church has not recognized a dichotomy between Jew and Gentile, the very premise upon which much of the premillennial dispensational system is built. Darby's "special revelation" from Ephesians that Israel and the church are dichotomous entities with distinct roles and relationships to God and Jesus Christ stands in sharp contrast to several New Testament passages that equate the church with the seed of Abraham.

> It is not as though the word of God had failed. For not all Israelites truly belong to Israel, and not all of Abraham's children are his true descendants; but "It is through Isaac that descendants shall be named for you." This means that it is not the children of the flesh who are the children of God, but the children of the promise are counted as descendants.
>
> —Romans 9:6-8

Now the promises were made to Abraham and to his offspring; it does not say, "And to offsprings," as of many; but it says, "And to your offspring," that is, to one person, who is Christ. . . . for in Christ Jesus you are all children of God through faith. . . . There is no longer Jew or Greek, there is no longer slave or free, there is no longer male and female; for all of you are one in Christ Jesus. And if you belong to Christ, then you are Abraham's offspring, heirs according to the promise.
—Galatians 3:16, 26, 28-29

In these verses, the apostle Paul clearly states that for those who have faith in Jesus as the Messiah, no distinction is to be made between Jew and Gentile. The two are now members of one family, the family of God, through Jesus Christ. In these verses, Paul builds on one of Peter's greatest achievements, which was to convince the Jerusalem council, who had criticized his association with the uncircumcised (meaning Gentiles), that "God has given even to the Gentiles the repentance that leads to life" (Acts 11:18), thus including Gentiles among the Jesus-followers for the first time. Consequently, the historical interpretation of the Christian church has been to conclude that not every detail of the covenant made to Abraham is to be literally fulfilled, as premillennial dispensationalism requires. Rather, those promises to Abraham accrue to believers who, though not ethnic Jews, have come to faith in Christ.

A half century or so after the last writings of the New Testament, the Apostles' Creed was formed. This is the basic creed for many Christian communions. The creed holds as one of its basic premises belief in the "holy catholic church." The word "catholic" here refers not to the Roman Catholic Church, but to the universal church of the Lord Jesus Christ. No distinctions are made in this creed between those of Jewish and Gentile descent. The universal church is inclusive of any and all who believe. The remainder of the creed contains a historic statement of the Christian faith.

I believe in God, the Father Almighty, the Creator of heaven and earth, and in Jesus Christ, His only Son, our Lord: Who was conceived of the Holy Spirit, born of the Virgin Mary, suffered under Pontius Pilate, was crucified, died, and was buried. He descended into hell. The third day He arose again from the dead. He ascended into heaven and sits at the right hand of God the Father Almighty, whence He shall come to judge the living and the dead. I believe in the Holy Spirit, the holy catholic church, the communion of saints, the forgiveness of sins, the resurrection of the body, and life everlasting. Amen.

While often in the current arena a "nonliteral" interpretation of Scripture is equated with liberalizing tendencies and thus, according to premillennial dispensationalists, denies the validity of the Word of God, the principle of literalness, when pressed in an unyielding manner, perverts the text.[21] Historically, the Christian church has embraced a variety of methods of interpreting Scripture and, for the most part, has recognized the need to accept texts on their own terms—that is, to allow the nature of a given text to guide its interpretation. For example, since prophetic oracles use a great deal of metaphorical and symbolic language, that symbolism is accepted rather than forced into a "literal interpretation." We will look more closely at and challenge premillennial dispensationalism's treatment of Scripture to support its notions in later chapters.

So what do we conclude? At the very least, when compared with historic orthodox (meaning accepted in contrast to heretical) belief of the Christian church, premillennial dispensationalism is built on the faulty foundation of the dichotomy between Israel and the church, as well as the rigid application of a literal interpretation of Scripture. It is from this faulty foundation that the majority of the fundamental characteristics of the system flow. Nevertheless, a pretribulationalist, futuristic, Darbyite version of premillennial dispensationalism is the system from which LaHaye and Jenkins are working, as evidenced in both their novels and their nonfiction writings.

Note my addition of "Darbyite" to the end-time terms that define the theological system of the Left Behind authors. This final term serves to complete my definition of LaHaye and Jenkins's perspective. Not all premillennial dispensationalists hold rigidly to the Israel-church dichotomy Darby created. Consequently, those who adhere to the totality of Darby's system are further distinguished, as Bible professor Pieters succinctly put it, as "a minority of a minority, teaching a millennialism which no Christian church has ever admitted to in its creed, and of that millennialism a special form which many of the wisest millenarians repudiate."[22]

Premillennial Dispensationalism and the Left Behind Series

Premillennial dispensationalists believe that the course of history and the sequence of events that will herald the end of the world as we know it are foretold with great specificity in the Bible. Therefore, many adherents of premillennial dispensationalism are preoccupied with end-time speculations and are committed to interpreting the symbolism found in what they refer to as "biblical prophetic literature" in light of—and as an explanation for—contemporary and/or future events. This perspective is obvious in the writings of LaHaye and Jenkins, as evidenced by the subtitle of their nonfiction book, *Are We Living in the End Times?* which reads, "CURRENT EVENTS FORETOLD IN SCRIPTURE . . . AND WHAT THEY MEAN." For further evidence, one need only flip to the back cover and read the question that asks, "Did you know that there are five times as many [Old Testament] prophecies concerning [Jesus'] second coming?" and goes on to tout, "You'll be amazed as you learn ours is the first generation that has the technology and opportunity to uniquely fulfill the many prophecies of Revelation."

That the authors' premillennial dispensational perspective guides the story line is apparent throughout the Left Behind series and can be demonstrated by a quick look at the final volume (book 12) of the initial series, *Glorious Appearing* (hereafter cited as *GA*). Here the main characters in the story listen attentively while the learned, recently converted Jewish scholars explain from the Scriptures (including the New Testament) who will be resurrected when and how various groups will be judged.

According to the narrative, the church was raptured by Jesus before the tribulation so that it could be adorned as his bride when Jesus returns to earth, a time known as the "glorious appearing" (*GA*, 366). Those who were "dead in Christ" were resurrected at the time of the rapture and ascended as a part of the church to the heavens. However, as the story goes, the rapture did not include the Old Testament saints (ethnic Jews, such as Abel, Enoch, and Abraham) who lived before the time of Christ and have been deemed faithful. The latter will be a part of the first resurrection, which is named "the resurrection of life," but the timing for those participating in the first resurrection will be based on whether they are Old Testament saints or tribulation martyrs (newly converted Christians), both Jew and Gentile, who do not come to faith until after the rapture and are martyred during the tribulation (*GA*, 359). The Old Testament saints and the tribulation martyrs will be resurrected in the interval between the glorious appearing and the initiation of the millennial kingdom (*GA*, 359–60).

Further, LaHaye and Jenkins present three times of judgment, each with a specific purpose that suggests that God holds different classes of people to different standards. They identify the judgments as: (1) the judgment of believers (the true church), (2) the judgment of the nations (includes the Old Testament saints, tribulation saints, Jews still alive at the end of the tribulation, and Gentiles still alive at the end of the tribulation), and (3) the final judgment (includes Satan, the fallen angels, and all unredeemed people of all time) (*GA*, 364).

Within these judgments can be seen several characteristics of premillennial dispensationalism. The first judgment takes place shortly after the "true church" has been raptured to heaven. The second judgment, the judgment of the nations (also called the Semitic judgment) will be held at the Valley of Jehoshaphat (which means "God Judges"). Here gloriously returned Jesus will restore the Jewish nation and judge the sheep, the goats, and the Brethren of Jesus. Gentiles will be judged on how they have treated God's chosen people. The Gentile Christians who honored the Jews are the sheep, and those who have not honored the Jews are the goats. The Brethren of Jesus are the Jews who have survived the tribulation and converted. The sheep and the Brethren of Jesus will remain in the millennial kingdom, where the Gentiles will be subordinate to the Jews. The goats, on the other hand, will first go to Hades, apparently a holding station, where they will wait for the final judgment, at which time they will be cast into the lake of fire (GA, 367–69). The final judgment, the great white throne judgment, will occur at the end of the millennial reign, at which time Satan, the fallen angels, and all the unredeemed from every age will be judged.

While there is disagreement on some of the fine points between the Left Behind authors and Darby's premillennial dispensationalism—for instance, LaHaye and Jenkins believe there will be more than 144,000 Jews who enter the millennial kingdom—it is obvious that the authors of the series approach their writing from within Darby's general framework. Jews are attached to the physical earthly kingdom, while the "true church" is raptured away to become the bride of Christ; and the resurrection of life is distinct for Jews and Gentiles, as are the judgments. The theological distinctions of premillennial dispensationalism have social and political corollaries as well. These are also apparent in the Left Behind stories. This ideological agenda has sobering implications for the contemporary church, so it is to a description and analysis of this social and political ideology that we now turn.

CHAPTER 3

The War Against
Secular Humanism

*Sociology, or social service as generally emphasized is, in its final
outworking, a black-winged angel of the pit. . . . Satan would
have a reformed world, a beautiful world, a moral world, a world
of great achievements. . . . He would have a universal brotherhood of man; he would eliminate by scientific method every
human ill, and expel by human effort every unkindness; he would
make all men good by law, education and social uplift; he would
have a world without war. . . . But a premillennialist cannot
cooperate with the plans of modern social service for these contemplate many years with gradual improvement through education as its main avenue for cooperation, rather than the second
coming of Christ.*
　　　　　　　—Eli Reese, *How Far Can a Premillennialist Pastor
　　　　　　　　　　Cooperate with Social Service Programs?*

Premillennial dispensationalists have long been engaged in a philosophical war against secular humanism and the social gospel. The
description of the battle has been addressed primarily to the
Christian church with the expressed aim of keeping the church
holy and pure. While this sounds like a positive agenda, it is necessary to look at the details of this effort and its assumptions before
assessing its value.

It would not be unfair to suggest that premillennial dispensationalists represent an ethnocentric subculture in the United States, and possibly around the world, complete with its own set of social and political agendas. They often oppose humanitarian and social justice efforts (each of which they equate with secular humanism), suggesting that such works to improve the lives of people and challenge unfair social structures represent the end-times apostasy (abandonment of the faith) described in the Scriptures. Simultaneously, premillennial dispensationalists have predicted the demise of democracy, suggesting it will lead to anarchy and thus pave the way for the Antichrist. According to this mind-set, attempts at creating a man-made utopia are nothing more than "the devil's cunning scheme for bringing in a mock millennium without Christ."[1]

While, in the grand picture, premillennial dispensationalists live in the world, they strive to be set apart from a world they consider to be held captive by secular humanism. Thus they adhere to an understanding of the relationship of the church to culture as "Christ against culture."[2] Living within this perspective, they may hold secular jobs, but they see resisting contemporary society and culture as part of the effort to remain "pure and holy" in preparation for the rapture. Holding the conviction that their narrow understanding is an absolute truth and a secret knowledge that many in the world will never understand, they see the world in terms of good and evil, right and wrong, with very few, if any, maybes. In contrast to other evangelicals, premillennialists have believed, per *The Scofield Reference Bible* writings, "the Gospel has never anywhere converted all, but everywhere has called out some."[3] Although premillennial dispensationalists have sought conversions, they have never believed the world would be transformed through the spread of the gospel. According to their belief, Christianization will come only when King Jesus has defeated all his enemies and is seated on the throne of David. In other words,

God's purpose for this age of the church is to gather the relatively few elect from the nations, rather than to Christianize the world.[4]

Premillennial dispensationalists believe they are the "true church" that will be raptured, while impure and unholy nonbelievers will suffer consequences by their own choices, since all have had the opportunity to hear and respond to the truth. All true believers must fall in line, tow the mark, and stay the course in order to be prepared for the rapture. Everyone has a role to play, and hierarchical safeguards are in place to protect people from straying. This premillennial dispensationalist hostility toward secular humanism and the social gospel, coupled with the endeavor to keep the church pure is vividly apparent in the thought of the authors of the Left Behind series.

Secular Humanism as Understood by LaHaye and Jenkins

LaHaye and Jenkins emphasize that the early church, from the time of the apostles up to the fourth century, held a premillennial view of future events. In doing so, LaHaye and Jenkins attempt to give credence to their claim that humanity's propensity for evil can only be remedied through the supernatural events surrounding Jesus' second coming. Consistent with this view is their understanding that the tribulation will force billions of people to choose between Christ and the Antichrist, thus sealing their fate for eternity.[5] While it may be true that the early church held a premillennial view, it is important to note they did not hold to the Darbyite perspective of the Israel-church divide. Thus their ideas about what would happen when Jesus returned would have been very different from those purported by LaHaye and Jenkins in the Left Behind series.

In a discussion of why a great tribulation period is necessary, the authors expound on what they understand to be the battle between true Christianity and secular humanism.[6] In 320 CE, Emperor

Constantine of Rome had what LaHaye and Jenkins consider to be a questionable conversion to Christianity. During Constantine's tenure as ruler of the Roman Empire, things changed dramatically for the Christian church. The persecuted Christian church first became the tolerated church, and then, under the leadership of one of Constantine's successors, Theodosius, Christianity became the official religion of the empire. LaHaye and Jenkins mark this era as the beginning of the church's shift into humanism. They accuse Constantine of opening up the faith to paganism by allowing Christians to simply rededicate pagan temples and rename statues as Jesus, Mary, and the apostles. They assert further that pagan practices, all of which flow from Babylon, "the mother of all false religions,"[7] began to infiltrate Christian thought and practice. These practices included prayers for the dead, making the sign of the cross, "worship" of saints and angels, institution of the mass, and "worship" of Mary.

Less than a hundred years later, the influential theologian Augustine came along with what the authors term a "brand of Greek humanism [that] introduced 'man's wisdom' along with 'God's wisdom'"[8] into the church. While Augustine's thought led to a further infiltration of the church by paganism, his spiritualizing approach to Scripture had the unintended consequence of removing the Bible as the sole source of authority. This marginalization of the Bible, coupled with the fact that the Scriptures were kept locked up in monasteries and museums, left Christians "defenseless against the invasion of pagan and humanistic thought and practice," and in the end, "the Dark Ages prevailed and the Church of Rome became more pagan than Christian."[9]

LaHaye and Jenkins continue, describing the Middle Ages (the fifth to the sixteenth century) as a time when Babylonian mysticism controlled the church and forty million true believers were martyred. This reference is to the persecution of pre-Protestant and Protestant Reformers in the fifteenth through sixteenth centuries. LaHaye and

Jenkins focus specifically on the persecution of the French Protestants known as the Huguenots, whom they claim to be equivalent to modern-day evangelicals. They suggest that the massacres of the Huguenots (1536) so alienated François-Marie Arouet Voltaire and Jean-Jacques Rousseau that these eighteenth-century philosophers became anti-Christian thinkers, promoting philosophies that laid the foundation for what is today called "secular humanism."

The following is a summary of the description of the rise of secular humanism given by the authors of the Left Behind series: All forms of pagan, false religion come from ancient Babylonian mysticism; Constantine introduced this idolatry into the fourth-century Christian church, and consequently the church was dominated by Babylonian mysticism until the time of the Reformation. When "true believers," namely Protestant Huguenots, began to rebel against the Babylonian mysticism of the Catholic Church in the sixteenth century, they were persecuted and martyred for their beliefs. This led to the development of anti-Christian, humanistic philosophies that have evolved into contemporary secular humanism. Were it not for true Christians, such as pre-Protestant heroes of the faith and reformers like the Huguenots, "Christianity would have been destroyed."[10]

LaHaye and Jenkins's interpretive walk through history is, at the very least, a gross oversimplification of church history. It is also laced with anti-Catholic rhetoric. Their analysis shows a tremendous naiveté about significant historical information, including Christian practices before Constantine, the development of the academic discipline named theology, and the major contributions made to Christianity by Augustine. In addition, it supposes that the events of history as they have presented them, void of any critical sociocultural analysis, were the cause for the "dark" in the so-called Dark Ages.

There were, in fact, plenty of problems in the Christian church before Constantine, including numerous heresies, such as several versions of Gnosticism, the roots of which lie in Greek philosophy and folk religion. The first three centuries were complex and complicated times. The church was growing and spreading, but it was not monolithic. A significant shift did occur in the fourth-century church, but it had nothing to do with the incorporation of Greek philosophy; rather, it was related to class. Once supported by the empire, the Christian church began to grow in prestige and power, thus attracting more and more members from the aristocracy.

Theology did not become a separate defined discipline until after the Protestant Reformation in the sixteenth century. And it was not until the seventeenth century that the term *biblical theology* came into use, building on the Reformer's emphasis on Scripture as the sole source and norm for matters of faith. Up until that time, all theological ideas came through the lens of philosophy. Any theological thought was understood as a part of the philosophical dialogue and intertwined with various philosophies depending on the region and time period in which it was created. Augustine, who wrote in the fourth century, like all the early influential theologians of Christianity (or "church fathers" as they are called), was understood to be a philosopher and used philosophy as the basis for the development of his belief system. Much of Augustine's work was and remains foundational for the Christian church, Roman Catholic and Protestant. One of the most significant of his writings is *The City of God*, in which he describes his hope of a truly Christian church and a truly Christian empire. This book was eschatological in that it looked toward and hoped for the kingdom that has no end, much like the hope professed by John of Patmos in the book of Revelation.

In recent years, the term *Dark Ages* has been replaced by *Early Middle Ages*, a time when the Roman Empire was in decline, suffering foreign invasions from all directions, poor climatic conditions, severe economic recession and inflation, and the onslaught of the bubonic plague and other epidemics from Asia. As Rome's power and population diminished, so did its ability to handle the administrative burdens of an overextended empire. Thus fewer records were kept, fewer contemporary histories were written (suggesting a dark, that is, unknown or silent, period). The empire suffered from an absence of material cultural achievement as well as a lack of Latin literature. In the midst of this decline, numerous manuscripts, including Scriptures, were taken to and held in monasteries for safe-keeping and preservation. The label Dark Ages has erroneously been thought to mean what is seen as the period's backwardness and extensive misfortune, a faulty notion that LaHaye and Jenkins perpetuate in their discussion.[11] For LaHaye and Jenkins to suggest that lack of access to the Bible caused the Dark Ages is absurd. Additionally, much of the population in this time period was illiterate and would neither have had nor benefited from firsthand access to the Scriptures.

Further, to suggest the Huguenots were the equivalent to today's evangelical Christians is a bit of a stretch. The Huguenots, whose predecessors were pro-reform Roman Catholics, followed Lutheran Protestantism and later adopted Calvinism, decrying the priesthood, the hierarchy, and the worship practices of Roman Catholicism. They accepted the belief that God's predestined mercy toward the elect was what made them fit for salvation, making it accurate to refer to the Huguenots as the new "Reformed Church." Because of the Huguenots' belief in salvation through individual faith without the need for intercession and in the right of individuals to interpret Scriptures for themselves, many contemporary Protestant churches and denominations claim the Huguenots' views as their heritage.[12]

Some of these groups are evangelical in the sense that LaHaye and Jenkins use the term, but many are not. While it may be said that premillennial dispensationalists are evangelical in nature, not all evangelicals are premillennial and dispensational. Consequently, it is best, for the purposes of this study, to keep in mind that LaHaye and Jenkins are a particular type of evangelical; they are

ultraconservative evangelicals who are often referred to as fundamentalists. The term *evangelical* came into use in the modern age[13]
to refer to groups of believers who support religious liberty and
consequently embrace a considerable variety of Christian traditions, all the while holding to their own distinctives. Evangelicals
are committed to the centrality of the gospel of Jesus Christ and the
necessity of its message preached to all peoples at all times.

Fundamentalism rose to notoriety in the 1920s and is characterized by belief in inerrancy of Scripture, the Virgin Birth, the mira-
cle-working power, atonement, and resurrection of Christ, and by
an emphasis on millenarianism.[14] Fundamentalists can, and often
do, refer to themselves as evangelicals, however, the term *evangelical* could also refer to someone who holds the gospel of Jesus
Christ as central but does not adhere to the basics of fundamentalism. LaHaye and Jenkins, as mentioned in chapter 2, are a minority within a minority.

Finally, to suggest a direct line between the martyrdom of the
Huguenots and contemporary secular humanism is an oversimplification of the events that took place in the sixteenth century as well
as of the development of thought into modern and postmodern
times. It is clear that conclusions of LaHaye and Jenkins about the
development of secular humanism are based on a faulty set of
assumptions and some bad interpretation of history.

Many things get lumped under the designation "secular humanism" by premillennial dispensationalists, and often secular humanists are accused of more things than are warranted. A basic definition, taken from the Council for Secular Humanism, may be helpful to our discussion.

> Secular Humanism is a way of thinking and living that aims to
> bring out the best in people so that all people can have the best
> in life. Secular humanists reject supernatural and authoritarian
> beliefs. They affirm that we must take responsibility for our

own lives and the communities and world in which we live. Secular humanism emphasizes reason and scientific inquiry, individual freedom and responsibility, human values and compassion, and the need for tolerance and cooperation.[15]

According to LaHaye and Jenkins, secular humanism is the nemesis of the true Christian church, which is built from all things spiritual with the Holy Spirit as the president. This negativity toward secular humanism flows from their commitment to what they understand to be a literal reading of the Bible set in contrast to human wisdom, as well as their fundamental belief that the human condition will continue to deteriorate until Jesus returns to establish his kingdom. This plays out in some spectacular ways, including an antithetical response to many of the expressed values of secular humanism. Premillennial dispensationalists like LaHaye and Jenkins suggest that any positive reform or advances made by human hands or through education alone are of Satan and can do nothing more than mimic the utopia that will exist when Jesus comes again. When the two ideologies are compared, it is clear that proponents of these diverse views share very little common ground and prefer not to associate with one another. While that is acceptable, since people have every right to choose with whom they will associate, what is not acceptable is LaHaye and Jenkins's depiction of secular humanism in the Left Behind series.

Secular Humanism and Roman Catholicism in the Left Behind Story Line

In *Tribulation Force*, Nicolae Jetty Carpathia, who is the Antichrist, is presented as a lifelong humanist who does not adhere to any religious creed. By portraying the Antichrist as such, LaHaye and Jenkins make a seriously negative rhetorical statement about secular humanism, even though, according to the statement of purpose quoted above, secular humanists function with a policy of tolerance, ethics, and cooperation as they seek to work for the well-being of all humanity. Although explicitly not adherents to a belief in the supernatural and therefore not religious in the traditional sense, it is hardly fair to identify secular humanists with the primary worker of Satan and the epitome of evil.

According to the authors' nonfiction work *Are We Living in the End Times?* as discussed above, the Roman Catholic Church has been controlled by Babylonian mysticism since the time of Constantine. This conclusion is based on their interpretation of the book of Revelation's use of Babylon as a metaphor for Rome (14:8; 16:19; 17:5; 18:2, 10, 21). Given their premillennial dispensational approach to the reading of the biblical text, if it says "Babylon," then it means Babylon (although Scofield understood Babylon to be metaphorical). However, when one reads the book of Revelation from a historical context, for example, "This calls for a mind that has wisdom: the seven heads are seven mountains on which the woman is seated" (Revelation 17:9), it is clear that John is using "Babylon" to refer to Rome, which is famous for its seven hills.

So the question remains: how does Revelation's use of Babylon to represent Rome lead to Babylonian mysticism in the Roman Catholic Church? The answer to this question has everything to do with the biblical interpretive method, which will be addressed at length in chapter 4. As futurists, the Left Behind authors interpret all biblical writings as predictions of future events and combine verses from various books of the Bible without regard for distinctions related to time, authorship, historical context, purpose, or theological perspective.

This interpretive method plays out in reference to Babylon and Babylonian mysticism, as follows: LaHaye and Jenkins read all references to Babylon in Daniel (Old Testament) and Revelation (New Testament) as being equal. Thus, when the author of Daniel refers to Babylon as the first of four world powers within his purview, the authors conclude that Babylon is the first world power ever to exist, overlooking Egypt, China, and Mesopotamia. This, however, is not what the book of Daniel is suggesting. Daniel's identification is in the context of world powers that have destroyed Jerusalem, and Babylon is the first world power to have done so. The notion of "world power" is also a matter of perspective. In antiquity, knowledge of foreign lands was limited to a particular geographical circle, since people seldom traveled beyond that circle and returned to report what they had found. For Israel, Babylon was a world power in that it dominated the totality of the geographical area with which Israel was familiar—the Ancient Near East—not including China, North and South America, much of Africa, and many other locales. This does not constitute the entire world as you and I know it today in which China, with a recorded history of nearly four thousand years, is understood to have been a world power long before Babylon enjoyed the title.

Prior to Babylon becoming a "world power," Assyria, whose heartland was located almost entirely within the boundaries of modern-day Iraq, held that position. During Assyria's reign, campaigns were made in all directions, and according to the biblical text, the northern kingdom of Israel was conquered in 722 BCE. Enemy attacks against Assyria interfered with the plan to conquer the southern kingdom of Judah, along with its capital, Jerusalem, and the temple, leaving Judah safe until 597/6 BCE when it became a vassal state of the world power of that time, Babylon. This arrangement continued for approximately ten years until King Zedekiah of Judah rebelled and in response Babylon entered Jerusalem, destroyed the city and the temple, and dispersed city officials throughout the Babylonian Empire.

In contrast, given their method of biblical interpretation, the Left Behind authors predict Babylon will be rebuilt into "New Babylon" in the twenty-first century so it can become the city from which the Antichrist reigns in the last days. Since, according to their interpretation of the Bible, Babylon is the first world power ever to exist, and since Babylon was the first empire to destroy Jerusalem, the authors conclude that Babylon is against the God of Israel, and, consequently, all that is bad has come through Babylon. "Every false religion in the world can be traced back to Babylon. . . . Satan had made that city his headquarters and introduced idolatry . . . and many of the religious practices that continue to the present day. These eventually appeared as the foundational teachings for Hinduism, Buddhism, Taoism . . . summed up in the Bible as "Mystery Babylon."[16] Thus, religious practices held by the Roman Catholic Church through the centuries, deemed by LaHaye and Jenkins as idolatrous, originated in Babylon and are therefore considered to represent a contamination of Christianity with Babylonian mysticism.

There are many problems with the LaHaye and Jenkins analysis of the Babylon of antiquity and the future rebuilt Babylon, which plays a major role in the Left Behind series. They say New Babylon, rebuilt by the Antichrist, is the city from which he rules the world, and it represents the final world power before the end of history and the coming of the kingdom of heaven. This final world power boasts a one-world government, a one-world economy, and a one-world religion. According to Left Behind, all of this will fall quickly into place once the rapture has occurred, for until then, the one-world government—and the end—are being held back by the presence of the true church. When the time has come—that is, when a predetermined number of true believers, defined as those who have kept themselves holy through the power of the Holy Spirit, has been achieved—the rapture will occur. Once people of faith in the one true God are snatched out of the world scene, the Antichrist, who is already poised for action, will begin his moves.

Stripped of the presence of true believers by the rapture, religious unity without respect for doctrinal differences becomes immediately possible in the world. This conclusion is based on the fact that in 1986 Pope John Paul II promoted unity among Christ-denying religions of the world by gathering 130 religious leaders in Iccese, Italy, to pray for world peace. LaHaye and Jenkins add to this "blasphemous" offense the contemporary cry for religious unity on the basis of tolerance and suggest that the only religious group not tolerated today is Bible-believing Christians.[17] Once the Bible-believers have been removed, the idolatrous worshipers of the world will unite to become the Babylonian harlot that will persecute and martyr the tribulation saints (those who have come to faith after, and in some cases as a result of, the rapture). LaHaye and Jenkins refer to the tribulation one-faith religious system as "Mystery Babylon," a name they create from John's reference to the mystery of the harlot in Revelation 17:5-7.

The religious scenario described above is played out in the Left Behind series through the character of Peter Matthews, a cardinal of more than ten years and a prominent archbishop of Cincinnati. In book 2, Matthews is elevated to pope of the one-world religion by the Antichrist, Nicolae Carpathia, after the former pope was raptured (this event suggests LaHaye and Jenkins believe some individuals in the Roman Catholic Church are true believers). The new pope's title is Pontifex Maximus, which he later (*Soul Harvest*) rejects to become Peter the Second.

In book 5, *Apollyon*, Matthews leads the Enigma Babylon One World Faith, which combines elements and symbols from every religion with no claims of exclusive truth. The only traditions not included are Christianity and Judaism, as they assert truth claims and are the ones being opposed and persecuted, for in the end, the real battle is against the one true God, the God to whom the Christians and Jews hold allegiance. In book 6, Matthews is murdered on suspicion that he is trying to overthrow Carpathia to become the ruler of the world, and Enigma Babylon One World Faith is replaced by Carpathianism, the worship of the Antichrist. While some extreme premillennial dispensationalists have identified the pope as the Antichrist,[18] the Roman Catholic Church is presented by LaHaye and Jenkins as a blasphemous bunch of idol worshipers and its leader as an unsuccessful Antichrist "wannabe".

This entire religious schema is based on the premise that once the "true believers" are gone, all the religions of the world will come together as one. Given our current worldwide religious tensions, it seems a bit unrealistic to predict such an occurrence. This prediction also presumes a mediocre commitment among other faith groups. Is it possible that the majorities of Hindus, Muslims, Buddhists, Taoists, and others are merely going through the motions and have so little commitment to their belief systems that they would immediately surrender to a one-world religion? Is it possible that the presence of Bible-believing Christians has enough worldwide influence and power to be the only thing holding people to their individual faith commitments? These suggestions border on the absurd and smack of ethnocentrism.

Religious ideas, practices, and worship styles are tremendously affected by cultural norms and standards. This is just as true for Christianity as it is for any other faith group. Christianity is described and practiced in different ways from culture group to culture group within the worldwide church, yet as long as the basic precepts of the Christian church, the most vital being the worship of Jesus as the Christ, are held, these expressions are authentically Christian. The challenge of acknowledging and affirming cultural differences as they are played out within our tradition isn't new. One of the apostle Paul's greatest contributions to the Christian church was when he, like Peter, broke through the ethnocentrism of Jewish culture to establish the Gentile mission (see, e.g., Galatians 3:28). This was no small thing. It was a monumental event filled with turmoil, angst, and tension; and as such, it stands as a model for each of us. But this model from Paul and Peter has not been emulated by LaHaye and Jenkins. The authors' attitude that their own race, nation, culture, and even gender is superior to all others is prevalent in their novels.

The ethnocentrism of the Left Behind novels is not limited to the religious realm. From the very beginning of the story, it is clear that the heroes and heroine are white people from the midwestern United States. The three main characters, Rayford Steele, Buck Williams, and Chloe Steele Williams form and are the leaders of the Tribulation Force, an organized group of believers who battle the Antichrist through the use of military arms and strategies that are supported by high-tech electronics. Initially the Tribulation Force was under the leadership of Pastor Bruce Barnes, who, soon after the rapture, became a world-renowned "prophecy scholar," not unlike Tim LaHaye.

After Barnes's death, the members of the Tribulation Force find thousands of pages of his writings and teachings, which they copy and distribute to new believers. Later in the series this role is taken over by Jewish scholars who have converted to Christianity. One of the fundamental precepts of the series is that the Jews have rejected God and are currently in a state of disobedience and rebellion, but since they are promised a special place in the kingdom, they will convert one by one until they reach a critical mass and must be housed at Petra for their own protection.

Meanwhile, the two heroes and one heroine are busy organizing tribulation saints into a worldwide co-op that provides protection, services, and goods as needed. Although the tribulation saints are found in every nation, it is clear the top leaders are the white males from the United States. Even heroine Chloe Steele Williams must take a backseat to the men.

Chloe's father, Rayford, and husband, Buck, are well-trained professionals at the top of their respective professions. Rayford, a Pan-Continental Airline pilot with an analytical, scientific mind, becomes the Tribulation Force leader after the death of Bruce Barnes and remains so through the end of the series, even when he moves to Petra (book 11, *Armageddon*). Tsion Ben-Judah, the leader of the Jewish community housed at Petra, insists that

Rayford continue as leader of the Tribulation Force with Tsion serving as chaplain. Rayford simultaneously serves, for a period, as the personal pilot for Carpathia.

Buck Williams starts out as the youngest-ever senior writer of the prestigious *Global Weekly*. More than one dozen of his stories have appeared on the front cover, and he has won several prestigious journalism awards. In book 2, Carpathia purchases the magazine and makes Buck the publisher of the newly named *Global Community Weekly*, giving insider access to Buck, who is the first to recognize that Carpathia is the Antichrist. Buck simultaneously publishes *The Truth*, an online magazine that counters the propaganda he publishes in Carpathia's magazine.

While the men, with their dual roles, can seemingly do anything and everything and go anywhere on a whim, Chloe is domesticated. Having no specific training or skills, she is kept at home as a support person much of the time, and eventually she has a baby (*Apollyon*), which further limits her activities. In one instance when Chloe does venture out on her own with positive results, she is reprimanded by her father for endangering the safe house (*Desecration*). For the most part, the women in the series are depicted in these domesticated and traditional roles, except for those who remain single.

Single women are frequently getting into or causing trouble in the story line. For example, Hattie Durham, Rayford's extramarital interest at the beginning of the series, eventually becomes Carpathia's girlfriend and ends up pregnant with his child. As she begins to see the evil in Carpathia, she contemplates an abortion. The Tribulation Force goes to tremendous efforts to stop her, but Carpathia discovers the pregnancy and has her poisoned. In the end, Hattie is brought to the safe house under the care of Buck and Chloe. She survives but loses her unborn child.

In the midst of this tremendous ordeal, which takes place over three volumes of the series, Hattie is repeatedly witnessed to by members of the Tribulation Force. She refuses to "accept God's forgiveness" because of the guilt she feels about all of her activities, but in the end, she comes to faith in Jesus and is visited by Michael the archangel, who sends her on a mission to speak out against the Antichrist when he appears at Golgatha (*Desecration*). Hattie, honored to be given such a mission, goes to Golgatha but barely speaks a word before she is consumed by fire from the sky. Several members of the Tribulation Force are surprised and jealous that Hattie is given such an honored role. Buck and Chaim, one of the Jewish leaders, witness Hattie's death and are inspired to boldly proclaim God's message.

Hattie's entire story reflects many social ideals of premillennial dispensationalism. Women who are not under the "headship" of solid Christian men are vulnerable and seemingly unable to figure out what to do. Consequently, they end up in trouble. While Hattie comes to faith, her martyr's death, for which, in *Glorious Appearing*, she receives a crystalline tiara and a "Well done good and faithful servant," is reminiscent of Palestinian suicide missions we so often hear about in current-day Israel. Is the call to martyrdom to be likened to a suicide mission? Or is there something much more profound to be understood about Christian martyrdom? This topic will surface again in chapter 5.

Another single woman, Verna Zee, is nothing but trouble for Buck Williams. Verna, initially Buck's supervisor, discovers that Buck is a Christian and threatens to reveal this information to Carpathia. When Buck becomes the publisher of *Global Community Weekly*, the tables are turned, but Buck does not retaliate and fire Verna, even though he discovers she is a lesbian. The Tribulation Force reach out and share their faith with her, but this only makes Verna think they are all odd. Buck's interaction with Verna Zee is suggestive of tolerance; however, she does not appear in the cast of characters blessed by God in the end. While Verna Zee is judged with the goats, who are consumed by the earth at Jesus' command (*Glorious Appearing*), Carmella, a fifty-year-old prostitute and drug addict, hears the gospel, becomes a believer, and consequently is blessed with the sheep, reinforcing the stereotypes that prostitutes and drug addicts are salvageable but lesbians are not.

Also reflective of stereotypes is the profile of Chang Wong. Chang is a believer who initially resides in China. Chang and his parents travel to New Babylon to attend Carpathia's funeral. At that time, Chang's parents force him to take the mark of the Beast. Chang becomes despondent over having received the mark but later discovers his parents had him drugged so that he couldn't resist the administering of it. Given that Chang has both the mark of the believer and the mark of the Beast, he is able to move back and forth between both worlds. Consequently, he works for Carpathia and for the Tribulation Force. Thus, he is a mole, and a high-tech mole at that. Chang is one of the computer whizzes on which the Tribulation Force depends throughout the great tribulation.

LaHaye and Jenkins pull no punches when it comes to Chinese religions. The characters of Chang Wong and his parents, along with the authors' interpretation of the sixth bowl of judgment from Revelation 16:12, provide evidence of the authorial team's prejudice against China. According to the interpretation, the kings from the east who will come to fight the Lord at the battle of Armageddon will include China, Japan, and all the Eastern nations. However, the authors predict that a power-hungry communist China will have already taken over all of Asia, as its recent demand for control over Taiwan and the Spratly Islands indicates. They believe China is the natural enemy who will march against the Lord on that final day, since China participates in the age-old worship of idols, pantheism, polytheism, astrology, and animistic humanism. In other words, China has been steeped in pagan religions for centuries and is currently controlled by humanistic communists with an obsession to control the world. Thus, they will be deceived into believing they can battle the Lord at Armageddon and win,[19] just as Chang Wong's parents were deceived into believing the best thing for their son was the administration of the mark of the Beast.

In the series, by the time the battle of Armageddon rolls around, the Antichrist is indwelt by Satan and is the world ruler with New Babylon as his capital city. The world is divided into ten regions, each with its own potentate. It is from these regions that Carpathia gathers two hundred thousand troops and sends them to the battle of Armageddon. However, the battle is fought instead at Petra, where the Tribulation Force leads the tribulation saints into battle against Carpathia and his armies, and Jerusalem, where Buck and Tsion Ben-Judah join the nonbelieving Jewish forces (*Armageddon* and *Glorious Appearing*).

Finally, LaHaye and Jenkins cannot resist adding some humorous touches to solidify their points. There are three characters named Aristotle, Plato, and Socrates in the story. The three Greek philosophers are working as a team in an attempt to discover the location of the Greek co-op. They are also captors holding George Sebastian, a vital member of the Tribulation Force, captive in Greece. Members of the Tribulation Force on a mission to free Sebastian are able to capture Socrates and force him to call in to Aristotle and Plato. In the end, George Sebastian escapes, the three philosophers are unsuccessful at raiding the Greek co-op, and the members of the Tribulation Force dismantle their plane with angelic assistance (*The Remnant*). The point is that the Greek philosophers (and Greek philosophy we may assume) are ineffective.

Conclusions

As self-designated literal readers of the Bible, LaHaye and Jenkins have done much more than interpret end-time biblical passages. They have used the premillennial agenda to declare what is good and what is evil, who is in and who is out, and how proper Christians ought to behave. According to these authors, secular humanism is the satanic nemesis of the true Christian church; the Roman Catholic Church is filled with idolaters; the Chinese are pagan humanistic communists plotting to take over the world; the world is quickly moving toward a one-world government, economy, and religion over which the Antichrist will reign; white U.S. American males will physically take charge and lead us to the path of salvation; Jewish men will convert to Christianity and teach that Bible prophecy speaks of Jesus; women play support roles, which includes the priority of bearing and taking care of children; the "other" is the enemy and is to be evangelized whenever possible; Greek philosophy has polluted Christianity; martyrdom is an honor; and taking up arms is part of the call. This is an awful lot for one fiction series to accomplish, and we have only just begun to scratch the surface.

The authors base these conclusions on their own reading and a peculiar method of interpretation of Scripture. Many reputable biblical scholars around the world disagree with some, if not all of, these conclusions based on their own readings and interpretations of the Bible. In the following chapters, we will unearth the interpretive methods used by LaHaye and Jenkins and show how these methods lead to distorted conclusions. Alternative interpretations of key biblical passages and books will also be offered.

CHAPTER 4

The Battle for the Bible

There is a narrow sense of understanding a language in which one may be said to understand a language when he knows the grammar, the literal meanings of terms, and even the meaning of idioms. Such understanding does not suffice for the understanding of the metaphors of the language. In addition one must know something of the linguistic conventions . . . and even of minor facets of the general culture.

—*Language, Thought and Culture,*
Paul Henle, editor

Every fall a new set of students enters my Introduction to the Old Testament course, and invariably, at least one student will come to me and say, "I really don't need to take this class, I already know the Bible." Having read the Bible is not equal to knowing the Bible. Reading the Bible is essential, of course, but the Bible is a very complex collection of documents from an ancient age and culture. In the United States today, and I dare to say in much of the world, the common method for reading has become one of direct application wherein a reader selects a passage, often at random, reads it through, and immediately sits back to contemplate how the text directly applies to today and to his or her life. This almost magical approach entirely disregards the realities of what the Bible is and what it means to read it with integrity. In the end, this method demonstrates disrespect for Scripture and replaces the authority of the Word with the authority of the reader's time, place, and needs. Scripture verses pulled out of their contexts and strung together can be made to say almost anything. Many bad interpretations have resulted from such a process—some of which have been downright devastating.

I know a man who believed in his heart of hearts that God could and would supernaturally heal anyone who simply had enough faith. Consequently, he decided that instead of going to medical doctors when he or a family member was ill, they would pray and believe that God would heal them. This man quoted many Bible verses in support of his belief, and he stood firm. As a result, one of his children lost his hearing due to the destruction of both of his eardrums by untreated water on the ear. It was only after intervention by family members that the child was taken to a physician who surgically reconstructed his eardrums. The child fell so far behind in his educational process that he never finished high school and, as an adult, still has a 20 percent hearing loss. One of the common accusations made by certain groups, who often refer to themselves as "Bible-believing," is that those who disagree with their understandings have abandoned the authority of Scripture in lieu of becoming culturally accepting. It seems that what they really mean by "authority of Scripture" is the authority of *their interpretation* of Scripture. This same population often claims to read the Bible "literally" or "literally whenever possible," which begs the questions, "Who decides when it is and when it is not possible to read the Bible literally?" and "What are the criteria for making those decisions?"

While the commitment to reading the Bible "literally" sounds good, it is at best unrealistic and at worst deceptive. Even those who make this claim recognize that biblical writing uses metaphors, similes, figurative speech, parables, allegories, poetry, and symbolism. Biblical interpretation is, therefore, as much an art as it is a science.

The Art of Reading the Bible

Language and communication represent a complex system that we use every day without even thinking about it. We are born into this system and assimilate it as we move through early childhood. In the end, using language for communication becomes second nature, and we take for granted these very complex skills—that is, until we are challenged to learn a new language or to read a difficult literary work. Reading and understanding Scripture represents an especially complex communication experience, which can be greatly enhanced by an awareness of certain realities about the Bible.

1. *The language of the Bible.* The Bible is an ancient text that was originally written in Hebrew, Aramaic, and Greek. Therefore, most readers rely on translations of the biblical text in their own modern languages. Translation from one language to another rarely involves a one-to-one correspondence of vocabulary, so translation requires interpretation that necessitates a working knowledge of expressions, figures of speech, and common metaphors, as well as speech patterns and cultural usages of both languages.

2. *The time and place of the Bible.* The Bible comes from the Ancient Near East. This means that the way it expresses things and the things it refers to are from a time and culture that are far removed from contemporary readers. So understanding biblical texts requires study of the time, place, and culture in which the texts originated.

3. *The time span.* The Bible was written over a period of more than one thousand years, during which the people of the Bible experienced numerous political, cultural, and theological shifts. A serious study of any given Scripture text requires exploring the particular time, culture, theological understanding, and social/political environment from which it comes. The diverse books of the Bible, therefore, cannot be read and interpreted in the same way.

4. *Type of literature*. Some texts in the Bible are stories, some are poetry, and others are letters. And some, such as the Gospels, prophetic speeches, and apocalypses (which we will look at in depth later in this chapter), are highly specialized types of literature that reflect a particular historical setting. When Bible scholars talk about Bible books and texts within books, they frequently refer to *genre*, a distinct class of material that is identified by certain characteristics and purposes. For example, poetry in the Old Testament isn't characterized by rhyme and meter but by phrases that repeat or develop a thought (known as parallelisms) and by metaphors taken from the early years of Israel's formation. In contrast, biblical narrative uses storytelling as a way to describe that formation.

5. *What readers bring*. Everybody reads any piece of literature from his or her own social location. Literally all of our previous experiences come with us as we open the Bible and begin to read. This means that we all—and there are no exceptions—read the Bible through the lens of our experiences, our expectations, and our own formed opinions. Throughout the remainder of this book, we will refer to these expectations and opinions as preunderstandings and presuppositions. While we are incapable of interpreting outside of the preunderstandings and presuppositions we hold, we are capable of being self-aware and strategic about how we engage them.

In short, the seemingly simple undertaking of reading any portion of the Bible really means navigating the intersection of three very distinct worlds: the world of the writer(s), the world of the text, and the world of the reader.

The World of the Writer(s)

While we cannot always determine who wrote a particular Bible text, knowing when it was written offers a great deal of help for understanding it. Fortunately, the general time period from which

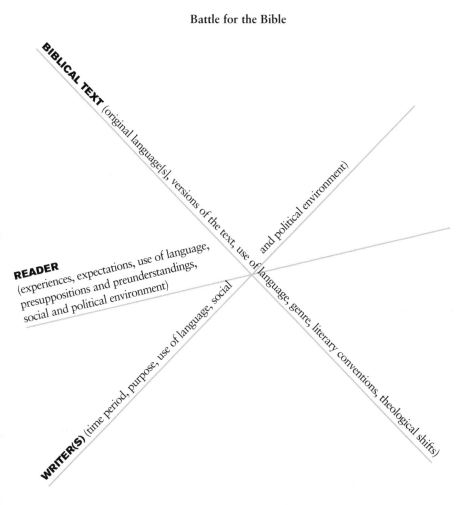

BIBLICAL TEXT (original language(s), versions of the text, use of language, and political environment)

READER (experiences, expectations, use of language, presuppositions and preunderstandings, social and political environment)

WRITER(S) (time period, purpose, use of language, social and political environment, genre, literary conventions, theological shifts)

a text comes can usually be determined. After that, the reader can begin to pursue questions that rise from the text about vocabulary, idioms, metaphors, cultural practices, and its social or political environment. For example, when reading the story of Judah and Tamar found in Genesis 38, it is helpful to understand the cultural practice known as levirate marriage, which required a man, under certain circumstances, to marry his deceased brother's wife. Without this understanding, a contemporary reader will likely impose his or her own ideals for family and marriage on the story and not understand why Tamar was "more in the right" than Judah (Genesis 38:26) when she seduced her father-in-law as he traveled on the road to Timnah (vv. 12-19).

Under the law of levirate marriage, Judah was obligated to give his third son to Tamar as a husband, but out of fear that this son would also die, he did not fulfill this obligation. Instead, he sent Tamar back to live with her parents, putting her in an impossible situation, since once she married Judah's first son, she became a legal member of Judah's clan. As a widow, she could not marry outside of the clan she married into, and if she were to attempt to do so, she would be killed.

These laws and customs were intended to protect family lines and inheritances in an age when there was no way to determine the paternity of a child. Also related was the need for a male heir from the first son, who was the primary inheritor of the father's wealth. When the first son died before Tamar could bear him a son, Judah's second son was obligated to marry Tamar to produce an heir who would be counted as the first son of his older brother. Judah's refusal had created two major problems: he had marginalized Tamar; and he had placed a roadblock in his own family line. Tamar understood these problems and took matters into her own hands to provide a male heir for the clan of Judah and to legitimize herself within her culture. This is why Judah said of Tamar, "She is more in the right than I."

The World of the Text

The fact that any given Bible text was originally written in ancient versions of Hebrew, Aramaic, or Greek can present particular challenges. For example, much of the Hebrew in the book of Job is very difficult to translate. This is in part due to the meaning of many words and phrases being lost in history and numerous words in Job being used only one time in the entire Bible. (Keep in mind that the original Bible texts did not come with dictionaries to help us understand the words and phrases, many of which mean different things in the modern versions of the languages.) So English readers will find that translations of Job vary considerably. Also, as mentioned above, it is very important to understand the genre or type of literature that the Bible book and a particular text represent and to ask, for example, "Am I reading from a gospel or a letter?" or "Is this text a poem or a folktale?" Of particular importance for our look at the Left Behind series and its interpretation of Scripture is how particular books of the Bible, such as Revelation and Daniel, use metaphors.

All literature contains metaphors, implied comparisons between two different things. For example, the expression "has a heart of stone," communicates not that somebody's heart is literally made of stone, but that the person lacks emotion and/or empathy. Since this is a familiar metaphor in our culture, we understand what is meant without thinking about it. Metaphors differ dramatically from culture to culture. For example, the phrase "chip off the old block," while common and meaningful in the United States, does not communicate well cross-culturally, especially when translated word for word. While we understand that it implies that an off-spring is like his or her parent, in another culture, the metaphor conjures up images of wood and wood chips.

Similarly, metaphors in the Bible are frequently confusing because they come from another time and culture. For example, the term *Zion* is used to refer to at least four different entities: the name of the fortress in Jerusalem (2 Samuel 5:7, 9), the temple mount (Psalm 132:13), the entire city of Jerusalem (Lamentations 2:6-8), and the people of Israel (Isaiah 51:16). The term connotes a whole range of concepts related to kingship, might, justice, the faithfulness of God, and security and well-being. Consequently, to understand the meaning of Zion in the Bible, it is necessary to first determine which of the four possible entities is being addressed and which connotation is intended.

Biblical texts also reflect shifts in theological understandings that take place throughout history. While God is the same yesterday, today, and forever, the human ability to understand and express God's nature is necessarily limited by human experience, thought, and language. The Old Testament contains descriptions of the people of Israel, their predecessors, and descendants, and their understandings of their identity and what it meant to be a people of God. The New Testament contains descriptions of Jews and Gentiles all striving to comprehend and express who they are, who God is, and what it means to be in relationship with God. Significant theological shifts and diversity of understandings are apparent throughout the Bible. For example, in the book of Joshua, Israel is commanded to kill all their enemies (11:12-15), while in the New Testament, Jesus commands his followers to love their enemies (Matthew 5:44).

The World of the Reader
Finally, as we read the Bible, we must be aware of the assumptions, expectations, and preunderstandings we bring to the text. In many ways, the world of the reader mirrors the world of the author, (see the figure on page 61). The preunderstandings and presuppositions that we bring to the Bible are formed within us by churches, pastors, teachers and parents; by personal experiences, political activities, cultural and social encounters, books, movies, and even music.

Part of becoming self-aware as readers includes recognizing our own use of idioms and metaphors, the social customs that we take for granted, and the political environments in which we live. These things affect not only the interpretations we arrive at, but also the expectations we bring and the very Scripture selections we choose to read. For example, the trauma and the drama of 9/11 affected Bible readers in several ways, including changing perspectives on national honor, enhancing the need to feel safe and protected, and altering views about if and when it is okay to engage in armed conflict. Passages or even books of the Bible that some people may not have been interested in reading before 9/11, for example, afterwards may have become a focus of study as they sought explanations and comfort. This was particularly evident in the surge in popularity of the book of Revelation, although people came to different conclusions based on their reading.

All too often we come to a biblical text with very strong feelings about what is right and wrong and true or false. Frequently these prestanding commitments overpower our ability to read the Bible as it is written. When this happens, it is we who become the authority, rather than the Bible. This happens particularly when people are committed to systems of belief and allow these systems to guide their interpretations. This then brings us back to the hot-button accusation by self-designated "Bible-believing literalists" that those who disagree with them have abandoned the authority of Scripture.

When someone accuses me of abandoning the authority of Scripture, I reply, "Right back at you." We are all guilty of this because we each read from our own location, because we cannot know for sure that we have comprehended the intended meaning of the author and, because as human beings, we all see in the mirror dimly (1 Corinthians 13:12). We therefore become dependent on "hermeneutical systems," or systems of thought, to help us in our reading. In reality, the accusation of abandoning the authority of Scripture rests on the assumption that the accusers' theological systems are biblically based, and therefore, anyone who interprets differently is not using their biblically based system. The real argument ought to be made at the level of systems of belief rather than as an argument about who is or is not "Bible-believing." What does the phrase "Bible-believing" mean, except that the Bible ought to be able to speak for itself, that the words of Scripture ought to be given priority for meaning? Perhaps an example will help to clarify.

In my Introduction to Old Testament course, I frequently give an assignment in which I ask students to do an analysis of the argument of Psalm 89, in which the psalmist makes several accusations against God. In verses 38-45, God is accused of renouncing the covenant even though God had promised never to do so (vv. 33-37). The psalm has very strong language, and the psalmist does not hold back from accusing God of reneging on promises. The words are clear, yet rarely is a first-year student able to make such statements about the psalm. They have in their minds, in the preunderstandings and assumptions they bring to the text, that God never lies, and it would be wrong to make such accusations against God. In fact, one student wrote that the psalmist was out of line in making such statements, because no one should talk to God that way. I read this section of the paper aloud to the class and presented this question: "Who is in authority here? Is it the Bible or the student who wrote the paper?" The student's preconception had preempted the authority of the Bible, allowing an existing belief system, rather than the biblical text, to determine what was right and true.

Given these realities—that the text reflects a culture and time from which we are far removed; that the languages of the original text are ancient, and in some cases translation is difficult if not impossible; and that we are all human, subject to mistakes, and we read Scripture through the trappings of our assumptions, experiences, and preunderstandings—how do we come to the Bible with any confidence that we can read and interpret with integrity?

Reading Scripture with Integrity

The critical question for each of us to ask ourselves as we approach the Bible is "What system of understanding do I bring to the text and why?" Everyone has a perspective from which he or she reads the Bible. The key is to know what it is, where it came from, and whether or not it is respectful of the history, nature, and authority of Scripture.

The Bible was written over a period of more than a thousand years, and the latest writings of the New Testament were written nearly two thousand years ago. Each book of the Bible was written in a particular time to a particular audience in response to a particular set of circumstances, so the writings had meaning for the community that first received them. Frequently this meaning was a word of hope that God was present with them and would deliver them from the impending harm they were facing, and many of these writings have been reinterpreted to bring a word of hope to a new time, a new day, a new generation, and a new set of circumstances. While interpretation and reinterpretation of the biblical text(s) is acceptable, encouraged, and even modeled in Scripture, reading Bible texts as if their messages were intended only for today is not. Critical to the enterprise of reading the Bible with integrity is acknowledging that the texts were written in response to particular times and circumstances. Only after readers have comprehended the biblical writings within their original time frame may they proceed to applying those same writings to their own time and situation.

This application involves the identification of truths that transcend time and culture to speak to contemporary situations. Not all aspects of any given biblical text have the potential for direct application. For example, the aforementioned concept of levirate marriage, while essential to understanding Genesis 38, cannot be transferred to contemporary U.S. American culture. Who among us would suggest that a woman is legally bound to marry the brother of her deceased husband? On the other hand, the principles of equity and justice for the disenfranchised, which are reflected in Genesis 38, hold much import for all cultures.

It is essential that readers of the Bible practice self-awareness and self-reflection. We can hold ourselves accountable for raising and researching questions related to date, sociocultural practices, political environs, and peculiarities of language. We can produce interpretations that are informed by an understanding of the author's world and the world of the text, and that are arrived at with an awareness of what we bring to the text. We cannot, however, claim to have fully comprehended the intention of the author. Those who claim to have determined the intended meaning of the author are seriously self-deceived. This point can be illustrated by a little exercise related to everyday communication.

Think of someone in your life to whom you are particularly close, say a spouse, child, parent, or good friend. Have you ever said something to that person, intending it to be positive, and had him or her become offended by it? Have your ensuing attempts at explaining what you really meant only enhanced the tension and misunderstanding? If we struggle to communicate with and comprehend communication from persons who live in our own time and culture, with whom we have close meaningful relationships, how much more difficult is it to understand communications from antiquity? We cannot and ought never to claim that we have fully comprehended the intended meaning of a biblical passage. At best we can catch a glimpse, and from that glimpse produce a meaningful interpretation for our own day.

Many readers will be wondering at this point about the inspiration of the Holy Spirit in the process of interpretation. People often refute the preceding principles for one of two different reasons. One is that they suppose they are capable of discerning the literal, authorial intent of a biblical passage through the power of the Holy Spirit. The other is their concern that the suggestion that a particular time and culture informs the writings of Scripture negates the Holy Spirit's guidance of the biblical writers. Both of these objections send us back to the concept of theological (hermeneutical) systems and in particular to the understanding of how the Holy Spirit works. How does the Holy Spirit help us to understand the Bible? Is guidance like having a ticker tape of words running across the mind? How did the Holy Spirit guide the writing of the Bible? Were sentences dictated so that the writers were nothing more than stenographers?

The answers to these questions will influence how any reader interprets the text, and reflection on these questions is an important part of becoming self-aware as we approach Scripture. Whatever the conclusion, there can be no doubt that Bible texts had meaning for and made sense to their first hearers and original audiences as well as to those who originated them. To suggest this is not true, or to suggest that portions of the biblical text were written only for those of us who live in the twenty-first century, is to negate God's work in the lives of those who first heard these words and in the lives of those who have turned to them throughout the centuries.

Questions related to the enterprise of biblical interpretation are numerous and could easily take one beyond the scope of this chapter. For now, let's return to our focus on the Left Behind series. If the glimpses of LaHaye and Jenkins's analysis of the end times seem complex and difficult to understand, there is good reason. Their end-time scenario is built from a multifaceted compilation of Scriptures, selected in light of their commitment to dispensationalism and a monolithic reading of the Bible, and interpreted with two crucial assumptions: that the fulfillment of most biblical prophecy is yet to come, and that the main focus of the Bible is to predict the second coming of Jesus. Bible scholars from a variety of theological perspectives, however, take issue with the base from which LaHaye and Jenkins are working. To lay the foundation for the analysis and critique of the authors' use of Scripture, we need to address the issue of genre as it applies to the books of the Bible that form the foundation of their thought.

Prophecy and Apocalypse

As mentioned above, one of the crucial steps to sound Bible interpretation is the determination of genre. Also of primary significance is dating, and the two—genre and date—often go hand in hand. This is especially true when Old Testament texts are quoted in the New Testament, which happens frequently and not surprisingly so, since what we call the "Old Testament" was the Bible for New Testament writers. In fact, much of the New Testament, as well as some of the Old Testament, is the reinterpretation of Scripture in light of new revelation, known in Hebrew as *midrash*. In other words, the New Testament writers were frequently reinterpreting their Scriptures (our Old Testament) in light of the new revelation that Jesus was "the Christ" (from the Greek word for "Messiah").

The analysis of the use of Scripture evidenced in the Left Behind novels necessitates our first identifying the two major types of material on which this end-time scenario relies, namely, prophecy and apocalypse. To discount the unique characteristics of either genre frequently leads to an interpretation that utterly disregards the meaning of the Scriptures for the faith community to whom they were initially addressed, which often results in creating a meaning for today that ignores the sociocultural issues and theological emphases of the setting in which the writing was completed.

Prophecy

Much of the churchgoing population today, if asked what prophetic books consist of, would answer "future prediction," but this would be incorrect. The majority of prophetic speech was focused specifically on how Israel and/or Judah were disobedient to the Law and thereby violated their covenant with God. Only after reviewing their unfaithfulness did a prophet move into a general word about the future. Typically this future word was about consequences should they not heed the prophet's call to change their ways and fulfill God's law and covenant. The best way to understand prophetic statements, then, is as a cry for reform.

The role of the prophet can be summarized as follows:

> Divine inspiration was what made a person a prophet, and what caused the prophet to speak out, and what made others listen to the prophet as a legitimate spokesperson for the divine. For the early period, a favored conception is that "the spirit of the Lord" speaks through the individual (e.g., 1 Sam

10:10; 1 Kgs 22:24). Later terminology preferred "the word of the Lord came to" the person (e.g., Jer 1:2, 4; Ezek 1:3). The general idea remains: the prophet is the one who can speak in the name of God.[1]

A prophet was an immediately inspired spokesperson for God, with the Spirit of the Lord speaking through, or the word of the Lord coming to, him or her. Prophecy is, therefore, primarily an oral genre. For the most part, prophets spoke their messages to the general population. The term "writing prophets" (Isaiah, Jeremiah, and Ezekiel, and the twelve minor prophets—Hosea, Joel, Amos, Obadiah, Jonah, Micah, Nahum, Habakkuk, Zephaniah, Haggai, Zechariah, and Malachi) simply refers to the fact that these speeches were eventually preserved in writing. A contemporary parallel would be a book of sermons that were originally presented orally and then were written down and compiled for publication. The word of the prophet was, as are sermons, meant to be heard by the prophet's community. And that word, which addressed the prophet's time and situation, represented an intersection of three lines of thought: the tradition of what it meant for Israel to be in covenant with God, their social and political situation, and the new word of God concerning the future. The message from the prophets of the Old Testament was a combination of forth-telling and foretelling, with forth-telling being the major component. Prophetic oracles specifically addressed the wrongs in the current culture and offered an explanation of what was happening at the time (forth-telling) and then ended with a general future prediction (foretelling) of hard times ahead should Israel not change, or in some cases, of a future hope in the midst of distress.

A significant problem in the contemporary Christian church is that many of us have felt the influence of premillennial dispensationalism in that we have been taught to read all things through the lens of Jesus. Consequently, we often approach prophetic books without regard for the original context of the material, because we understand the word *prophetic* to mean "a description of how Jesus is working in my life (my church, my nation, or my world) today." The idea that all of the Bible points to the coming of Jesus has taken over our ability to read the Old Testament as the first testament. This is not to discount the New Testament or what the New Testament writers say about Jesus. The New Testament writers were leaning on their tradition, what we call the Old Testament, to describe, define, and legitimate their understandings of Jesus.

For example, one assignment my students often struggle with involves studying Isaiah 7:14, which reads, "Therefore the Lord himself will give you a sign. Look, the young woman is with child and shall bear a son, and shall name him Immanuel." Having heard numerous sermons and participated in Nativity plays that interpret this verse as a prophecy of the birth of Jesus, it is difficult for them to accept the idea that the prophecy was originally spoken to offer assurance to a particular people in antiquity. Reading Isaiah 7:14 in its scriptural context reveals that the word was spoken to King Ahaz as a sign that God would be with him and with the nation of Judah (*Immanuel* means "God with us") in the face of an attack by Aram and Ephraim, promising that by the time the prophesied child was weaned (about two years old), the lands of Aram and Ephraim would be deserted, having been destroyed by the greater enemy, Assyria. Isaiah's prophecy, therefore, had significance and meaning for the first hearers.

This verse is later used by some of the New Testament writers to speak about Jesus, because they believed that, similarly, Jesus was a sign that God was with them/us, offering the same assurance that was given to Ahaz and his people. The New Testament writers were not in any way negating the prophecy given to Ahaz. Rather, they were using something known within their community, namely, the idea of Immanuel/God with us, to explain who this Jesus was. This of course is not the only instance where prophetic verses and expressions are used to speak about Jesus in the New Testament. And in each case, these texts have meaning in both the Old Testament and the New Testament, providing comfort (or warning) to the people of that day and doing the same for the Christian church today.

So when we study the prophetic literature of the Bible, it is important to know the time period from which it comes. Prophecies that were given prior to the destruction of Judah by Babylon in about 586 BCE focus primarily on social ills, impure worship practices, and the evils of non-Israelite nations. Prophecies given during the time when the people had been conquered and some of them exiled throughout the Babylonian Empire provided a theological interpretation of this exile as well as hope for restoration of Judah. And prophecies given after the people who had been carried away into Babylonian exile were allowed to return to Jerusalem (by decree of Cyrus, King of Persia in 538 BCE; Ezra 1:1) focused on the internal theological and political struggles related to the structure and practice of worship and the rebuilding of the temple.[2]

Apocalypse

An important first step for the study of biblical apocalyptic literature is a definition of terms, since in popular culture many terms have become distorted. While the word *apocalypse* in popular use has come to mean a cosmic disaster, the word actually means "an unveiling" or "an uncovering of something that was formerly hidden." An apocalypse, or "revelation," as the word is often translated, is a disclosure of previously hidden things.[3] The word *apocalyptic* is an adjective and *apocalypticism* refers to the belief structure of a movement that shares ideas typically found in apocalypses. Finally, the term *apocalyptic eschatology* refers to the attachment of apocalyptic ideas to the end of history, which often emphasizes the theme of judgment after death, which is not found in the prophets.

The key to this study is a sound understanding of the genre of biblical apocalypse.[4] As written pieces of literature, apocalypses, unlike prophecies, were not given first as oral sermonic presentations. Rather, they were written first, although they were most likely intended to be read aloud and interpreted to the people to whom they were addressed. Apocalypses are complex, filled with complicated symbolic language, and therefore not easily understood when given orally. A piece of writing is identified as apocalyptic by very distinct and identifiable characteristics and a particular worldview (see below). An apocalypse was mediated to a human recipient by an otherworldly being, usually a messenger from God (which is the meaning of the word often translated as "angel"). The messenger instructed the human recipient to write down all of the things he or she was about to hear or envision. It was not unusual for the human recipient to request an interpretation of the message due to the complex symbolism involved. The content of an apocalypse, then, is not of this world but represents a disclosure of a reality from another world (the heavenly world). It is focused on the end of the earthly reality as people know it and depicts a supernatural world in which those who are saved (often referred to as "the righteous") will participate.

Nine elements of the worldview behind biblical apocalypses are:

1. An ongoing tension between chaos and creation in which the current world order is typically presented as chaotic and in need of re-creation.

2. An expected future new creation that will not be of this physical earthly world but of another world that we cannot currently envision or imagine.

3. A dualistic worldview of good and evil in which there are two independent forces: God, who is good, and Satan, who is evil, in contrast to the earlier Old Testament belief that *all things*, good and bad, come from God.

4. A pessimistic view of the present world order that considers the present era so evil that there is no hope for reform and anticipates a sudden and violent imposition of God's rule.

5. An almost despairing view of human beings as so fundamentally defective and weak that the only hope is salvific intervention of God.

6. A democratization of the prophetic mission so that the focus is no longer on one prophetic leader. All members of the community to which this message is addressed are called to participate.

7. A belief that the nation of Israel and the elect are no longer one and the same.

8. A focus on individual resurrection or immortality and the concepts of hell and eternal punishment.

9. The former theology of history and traditional wisdom that characterized Israel's belief system replaced by special revelation or "wisdom from above" that reflects the need to understand larger cosmic realities.[5]

Apocalyptic literature, therefore, is a unique genre that has a set of characteristics that distinguish it from biblical prophetic literature. While prophecy is primarily oral, first spoken, then written, the apocalypse is primarily written. In contrast to the prophet, who was an immediately inspired spokesperson, receiving the message directly from God, the writer of the apocalypse received the message through an other-worldly mediator. And finally, while the prophet's word addressed his current time and situation, an apocalypse describes the end of the world as it is known and anticipates a futuristic new creation that will replace the current social order. In other words, the prophet's message was a cry for the people to reform while the apocalypse looked for the supernatural entrance of God into history to judge the world, to destroy evil, to save the righteous, and to create a world order marked by peace, justice, and equity.

As noted above, the Bible contains fifteen books that are categorized as "prophetic." Listed within the generic category of apocalypse are Daniel and Revelation. There are, however, apocalyptic sections found in other biblical books, such as Isaiah (chaps. 60–62, 65–66), Ezekiel (chaps. 38–39), and Mark (chap. 13). There are also prophetic sections in Daniel (11:40–11:45), and Revelation is actually a combination of prophecy and apocalypse, which, as we will see later, adds to the complexity of this commonly misunderstood biblical book.

Most scholars would place apocalyptic literature in the category of crisis literature, written in response to severe persecutions experienced by communities of faith. Certainly the books of Daniel and Revelation fit this designation. While the prophets tended to interpret enemy attacks as God's discipline for unfaithfulness, the biblical apocalypses interpret attacks as the wicked assaulting the righteous, even when they acknowledge the sin of the people. Consequently, instead of preaching for reform, the apocalypses record hope-filled visions of divine intervention that brings judgment for the wicked and salvation for the righteous. As we proceed down the path of reviewing interpretations that are foundational to the Left Behind series and developing alternative perspectives, it is important to keep in mind two fundamental tenets: (1) Each genre has its own unique characteristics that must inform the reading, and (2) all biblical books were written in the midst of and in response to a particular set of historical circumstances, the knowledge of which is critical for understanding them.

CHAPTER 5

The Biblical Books of Daniel and Revelation

The word "apocalyptic" is popularly associated with fanatical millenarian expectation, and indeed the canonical apocalypses of Daniel and especially John have very often been used by millenarian groups. Theologians of a more rational bent are often reluctant to admit that such material played a formative role in early Christianity. . . . Whatever we may decide about the theological value of these writings, it is obvious that a strong theological prejudice can . . . make it difficult to pay enough attention to the literature to enable us even to understand it at all. It will be well to reserve theological judgment until we have mastered the literature.
—John J. Collins,
The Apocalyptic Imagination

The end times scenario presented in the Left Behind series is drawn from premillennial dispensationalism. This guiding theological frame work, in turn, depends heavily on a futuristic interpretation of the biblical books of Daniel and Revelation. It is important then that readers become familiar with foundational information about these biblical books in order to understand the critique of LaHaye and Jenkins that is undertaken in chapters 6 and 7 of this book. Let's begin with Daniel.

Daniel

In the previous chapter, we introduced the literary genre known as apocalypse. Two major types of apocalypses can be found in biblical material—historical apocalypse and otherworldly journey apocalypse. Historical apocalypse is characterized by the use of visions and an interest in the development of history. Daniel is a historical apocalypse that was written somewhere between 167 and 164 BCE. LaHaye, Jenkins, and other dispensationalists insist that Daniel was written much earlier. This conclusion is based on a "literal" reading of the first six chapters of the book, which contain the content that is most familiar: the stories of Daniel's three friends Shadrach, Meshach, and Abednego being thrown into the fiery furnace; of Daniel and the lion's den; and of King

A Brief Outline of the History of the Kingdom of Israel
- The United Kingdom under David and Solomon (1000–922 BCE)

- The kingdom divides into north (Israel) and south (Judah) (922 BCE)

- The northern kingdom (Israel) falls to the Assyrian Empire (722 BCE)

- The southern kingdom (Judah) falls to the Babylonians and suffers two deportations of its population throughout the empire (597–587 BCE)

- The Persian Empire and the return of the exiles and rebuilding of the temple (538–336 BCE)

- Empire of Alexander the Great, and Palestine under Egyptian control (336–323 BCE)

- Palestine under control of Seleucids (198–63 BCE)

- Rise of Roman Empire and Roman occupation begins (63 BCE)

Nebuchadnezzar's dream. It is possible that these stories came from the Babylonian exile or "the diaspora" of 597 to 538 BCE (or even the time of Persian rule; (see p.78), during which a significant portion of the population of the southern kingdom of Judah was deported and spread throughout the Babylonian Empire. These stories, known as "diaspora tales," were written to provide a model of Jewish faithfulness for those living in a strange land under oppressive conditions.

These diaspora tales were used by the writer of Daniel to form the introduction to his apocalypse, which makes up the rest of the book. The book of Daniel is generally dated by scholars according to the historical outline found in chapters 7–11, which are historically accurate through verses 40–45 of chapter 11. Antiochus Epiphanes IV was the third and most destructive Seleucid monarch to control Judea. Daniel 11 describes his campaigns and predicts his death (vv. 40-45). He died in 164 BCE, but not in the manner predicted in Daniel. Consequently, it has been concluded that chapters 7–12 of Daniel were written prior to the death of Antiochus, sometime between 167 and 164 BCE.

While those who claim an early dating for Daniel insist that chapters 7–12 are "prophetic," as in predictive of future events, it is important to keep two things in mind. First, Old Testament prophecy is not primarily prediction. As outlined in chapter 2, prophecy confronts the social and religious ills of the day, cries for reform, and foretells by warning of dire consequences if reform is not undertaken or by providing general words of hope. Second, Daniel is not a prophetic book; it is an apocalypse. Historical apocalypses are all about reviewing and providing a theological interpretation of history as well as offering general hope for the future. In the end, they may or may not provide a prediction of specific impending events, such as the description of the death of Antiochus Epiphanes IV in Daniel 11:40-45. The curious thing is that Daniel 11:40-45 was retained and put into the Bible even though it is clearly a "false prophecy." Retaining an inaccurate prophecy and placing the book in the canon only makes sense when we recognize that the book was understood as something other than prophecy, as an apocalypse. In fact, those who compiled the Hebrew Bible grouped Daniel not with the prophets but in a section called "the Writings." This section also includes Psalms, Ruth, Esther, Job, and some later historical books. More important to our discussion, however, is the main message of the book of Daniel, which flows from recognizing it as a credible apocalypse from the second temple period.

The second temple period began in 538 BCE when the Jews returned from exile and began rebuilding the temple in Jerusalem, which was completed around 515 BCE. This era ended with the destruction of the temple in 70 CE. During this time, apocalypses were frequently written in response to moments of severe crisis. Daniel is one of several books written in response to the crises imposed on Jerusalem by Antiochus Epiphanes IV from 175 to 164 BCE. These crises began with the replacement of the high priest Onias III with his brother, Jason, who secured the position by paying Antiochus IV a large sum of money. This change meant that the highest-ranking official in Judaism became a direct appointee of the foreign overlord. As high priest, Jason opened wide the doors of the temple, allowing Antiochus opportunity to plunder and desecrate.

In 167 Antiochus IV decreed that the whole kingdom should be one people and that the Jews would no longer be allowed to follow customs strange to the Greek world. The people were commanded to build altars and shrines for idols. The temple was renamed for Olympian Zeus, and Jews were forbade to worship their God. Turning the temple of God into the temple of Zeus presented a horrible crisis for the Jews because it cut to their religious and cultural core. The command to worship Zeus meant heresy, an abomination to the one true God, and something they could never agree to do. To enforce his decrees, Antiochus IV built a stronghold in Jerusalem and charged the soldiers stationed there to kill any Jew who disobeyed this new decree.

The books of Daniel and 1 and 2 Maccabees are in response to the crises that arose under Antiochus's reign. First and Second Maccabees are historical books found in the Apocrypha, which is a group of books that are included in the Greek edition of the Hebrew Bible and in the Latin translation of the Hebrew and Christian Scriptures but were not included in the official Hebrew canon or in the Protestant Bible. Daniel and the Maccabees represent two very different responses to the same crises. The Maccabees provide a description and theological interpretation of a Jewish revolt led by Judas Maccabeus and his family against the decrees of Antiochus Epiphanes IV. In the end, the Maccabees were able to regain control of Jerusalem and the temple in 164 BCE, and they were able to retain that control for about a hundred years. First and Second Maccabees calls the Jewish people to violent resistance.

In contrast, Daniel calls the people to nonviolent resistance, even to the point of death.

Although chapters 1–6 and 7–12 of Daniel contain different genres, they are quite connected, as the entire book is focused on living as a faithful Jew under foreign rule. In the diaspora tales of chapters 1–6, Daniel and his three friends are able to remain faithful to Jewish law and, like Joseph before them (Genesis 37–50),

Outline of Daniel

Chapters 1–6: The Diaspora Tales
1 Introduction of Daniel and his friends
2 Nebuchadnezzar's dream
3 The fiery furnace
4 Nebuchadnezzar's madness
5 Belshazzar's festival
6 Daniel in the lion's den

Chapters 7–12: The Apocalypse
7 The vision of the four beasts
8 The vision of the ram and the male goat
9 The prophecy of the seventy weeks
10 Prologue to the vision of the last days
11 The vision of history unfolding
12 The final consummation

become successful in a foreign land. Throughout the story, Daniel and his friends' commitment to Jewish law is challenged over and over, but in every instance the four remain faithful. Their reward is deliverance from the sentence of death, a heightened status in the court, and a proclamation by the king that their God is the one true God. These stories make the point that, although life in a foreign land has its threats, those who remain faithful to God will be delivered and will eventually prosper.

In Daniel 2 strong emphasis is placed on the four world powers—the Babylonians, the Medes, the Persians, and the Greeks—that ruled over the Jewish people throughout the centuries. This story was designed to instill hope and to encourage the Jews to remain faithful while looking forward to the time when the oppressor of the day would be destroyed by the fifth kingdom—the indestructible kingdom of God on earth. In contrast to some earlier historical books, such as 1 and 2 Chronicles, Ezra, and Nehemiah, and in keeping with the character of apocalyptic writing, the hope expressed here looks toward a time when God will establish a new kingdom, rather than toward the reestablishment of the Davidic monarchy.

The apocalypse in chapters 7–12 also focuses on the four world powers of Babylon, Media, Persia, and Greece. In chapter 7 the kingdoms are depicted as four awful beasts rising out of the chaotic sea. The final beast sprouts ten horns. These horns represent the ten rulers who follow the death of Alexander the Great. Then an eleventh horn appears, and to make room for it, three horns fall off. This eleventh horn represents the rule of Antiochus Epiphanes IV, who displaced three rulers when he came into power. This eleventh horn speaks arrogantly, which is an allusion to the desecration of the temple by Antiochus in 167 BCE. Immediately following the eleventh horn comes the Ancient One who takes a seat on the throne. The Ancient One sits in judgment, and consequently Daniel sees the fourth beast put to death. The arrogant horn has been silenced. Then coming in the clouds is one like a "son of man" (v. 13 NIV), who is given dominion, glory, and kingship so that all the nations should serve him. His dominion is eternal and his kingship shall never be destroyed (v. 14). The scene depicts the arrival and establishment of the kingdom of God.

The remainder of the book of Daniel reiterates the opening scenario of chapter 7, using different imagery and differing emphases. The end of chapter 8 describes the horrors that Antiochus IV imposed on the Jews in Jerusalem during his reign. Daniel's response comes in the form of a prayer of confession for his sins and the sins of the people (Daniel 9), indicating that the persecutions wrought by Antiochus IV were understood as discipline or punishment brought on by the sins of the people. Nevertheless, the chapter ends with the word of hope that seventy weeks have been decreed for the punishment, after which the end will come and the desolator (Antiochus IV) will be destroyed (9:27). Verses 24-27 of Daniel 9 are very important to the premillennial dispensational time line, as will be discussed in chapter 6.

Chapter 10 begins with Daniel standing on the bank of the Tigris River with a group of people. When Daniel looks up, he sees a vision of a man who turns out to be a messenger of God. The messenger tells Daniel his prayers have been heard since the first day he set his mind to gain understanding of what was happening (v. 12) but that he had been delayed because he had been fighting against the prince of the kingdom of Persia. This explanation highlights an important theological worldview held by many during the second temple era that is reflected in apocalyptic literature. It was thought that the real battles between political powers were fought in the heavens and that the wars on earth were mere reflections of these cosmological battles. The heavenly warriors were the cosmological creatures assigned to each city-state as overseer and protector, often Michael for the Jews (see v. 13). The message Daniel receives from this visitor is found in chapter 11. This message is the description of the reign of Antiochus Epiphanes IV, with the exception of verses 2-4, which describe the end of the Persian Empire and the rise and fall of Alexander the Great, and concludes, as noted above, with an inaccurate prediction of Antiochus's death.

It is important to note that in each chapter's (chaps. 7–11) description of the rise and fall of the four kingdoms that lead up to the climactic death of Antiochus Epiphanes IV, the emphasis on the earlier kingdoms is progressively reduced, while the descriptions of the rule of Antiochus IV are progressively increased. This shift serves to emphasize the climactic events that take place at the end of the reign of Antiochus IV that were predicted to usher in "a time of anguish, such has never occurred since nations first came into existence" (12:1). But hope is offered: "everyone who is found written in the book" will be delivered, and "many of those who sleep in the dust of the earth shall awake, some to everlasting life, and some to shame and everlasting contempt" (vv. 1-2). These verses contain the only clear reference to the resurrection of the dead to be found in the Old Testament.

The book of Daniel closes with two predictions about the length of days till the end of the persecution and the beginning of the fifth and final kingdom: 1,290 days (12:11) and 1,335 days (v. 12). No one knows for sure why there are two predictions. Whatever the case, the apocalypse of Daniel ends with a word of hope to those facing persecution for their faith: "But you, go your way, and rest; you shall rise for your reward at the end of the days" (v. 13).

Revelation

The contemporary church has received numerous and variant interpretations of the book of Revelation. It is quite possible, in fact, that today's Christians have heard so many different ideas about this biblical book that they are at a loss as to where to begin to understand it. Revelation is one of the most complicated books in the Bible. The book is not a straight read, and it must be approached with an eye toward the writer's artistic storytelling, which seeks to persuade hearers through creative use of biblical and cultural images.

The story line is complex and confusing as it flashes forward and backward and shifts from one judgment to another, making it difficult to determine how much repetition and overlap the book contains. For example, there are three sets of seven judgments in Revelation, of which the first two are interrupted with some type of interlude, and the third is delayed by a description of a conflict between Satan and the church that had to have taken place before the first judgments (chaps. 12–14). Once the final judgment has been made (16:17-21), the text then flashes back to a description of the destruction of Babylon (chap. 17), followed by a lament for that city and rejoicing in heaven over its destruction (chaps. 18–19). Then comes the battle between Jesus and the Antichrist and his False Prophet (19:17-21), followed by a thousand-year internment of Satan (20:1-3) and the appearance of a new Jerusalem (chap. 21).

Revelation is overwhelmingly characterized (over 275 of the book's 404 verses) by indirect references to or slight mentions of other biblical books. In addition to these allusions, the book uses parody to emphasize the playoff between good and evil. All that is good is mimicked by evil ones. Hearers/readers are confronted with a call through these parodies not to be deceived by evil but to remain faithful to the true God. The writing in Revelation also capitalizes on outlandish imagery of the day, which is generally unfamiliar to contemporary readers. These depictions are consistently built from a conflation of several biblical and popular images. By combining images that are familiar to his readers/hearers, the writer emphasizes particular aspects of various characters and events.

Some of the language of Revelation that may appear straightforward is clearly not meant to be interpreted literally. This is especially the case with numerical references and periods of time. For example, Revelation 17:9-14 speaks of ten kings who are represented by ten horns on the seven heads of a beast who came from the sea and who will each reign for "one hour" (v. 12).

A final complicating factor is that many contemporary Christians have been affected by premillennial dispensational interpretation of the book of Revelation. The partial influence of this system of belief, when blended with numerous ideas from other fronts, leads to mixed-up understandings of the book. Finding our way to an integrated interpretation of the book called "Revelation" necessarily means beginning with questions of authorship, genre, purpose, date, and historical context.

Background

The book of Revelation identifies its author as a man named John. John was a common name in New Testament times, and it is likely that the book was written by a John other than the one associated with the Gospel of John. The tone, content, and focus of Revelation are quite distinct from the Gospel. The Gospel was written in part as a response to attacks by Jewish religious leaders against the messianic claims concerning Jesus. This purpose contrasts with the major focus of Revelation, which is to confront the persecution of Christians by Rome. Revelation depicts Jesus as the one coming who will gather his own unto himself, while the Gospel of John seeks to explain the mystery of the person of Jesus and his divinity. All we know about the John of Revelation comes from four verses of the book where his name is mentioned: he testified to his faith in and knowledge of Jesus the Christ (1:1); he received a vision from Jesus the Christ (22:8), which he has passed on to seven churches through letters and to the larger community through the written work we call "Revelation" (1:1, 4); and he was persecuted and exiled to the island of Patmos because of his testimony of Jesus (1:9).

The first word in the book of Revelation is the Greek *apokalupsis*, which means "revelation" or "unveiling"; thus the book introduces itself as an apocalypse. This genre identification is borne out by the fact that the message to John comes in the form of a vision mediated through an angel. As noted earlier, there are two types of apocalypses: the historical apocalypse and the otherworldly journey apocalypse. In Revelation both types are woven together. While, as in the historical apocalypse, the book reflects and explains a particular time period and set of events, it also describes the writer's journey to and visions of the cosmos and places of judgment, which is characteristic of the otherworldly apocalypse.

Portions of Revelation are also referred to as "prophecy," and in these sections John is called to prophesy (1:3; 10:11; 19:10; 22:7, 18, 19). Within the first eight verses of the book are found two prophetic words that John has received directly from God (1:7-8), and a series of prophetic sayings appear just before the conclusion of the book (22:6-20). In this complex book, the prophetic and the apocalyptic have been fused together to create a very unique literary work. But that's not all.

Apart from the preface (1:1-3), Revelation has the appearance of an ancient letter, much like those written by the apostle Paul. The formal characteristics that suggest it is a letter include a salutation (1:4a), a greeting (1:4b-5), a doxology (1:5b-6), and a concluding blessing (22:21).

Revelation, then, is not typical anything. It is not a typical apocalypse, not a typical prophecy, and not a typical letter. The structure, which is an intricate interweaving of these three major genres, adds to its complexity. This complexity is a sign of things to come.

One of the mistakes often made in reading Revelation is neglect of its historical context. It is this context that provides the keys to its interpretation. Most of the images in the book, for example, relate specifically to entities that existed in the time of its writing, one instance being the use of Babylon as a code name for Rome.[1] To miss this correlation is to miss the main focus of the book. John was exiled by the emperor of Rome to the island of Patmos because of his commitment to the Jesus movement, and it is because of persecution—past, present and anticipated—that he writes this message of encouragement to the Christian churches in the empire. While most scholars suspect that John completed Revelation toward the close of the reign of the Roman emperor Domitian (81–96 CE), some date the book closer to 70 CE, when the second temple was destroyed by Roman armies. In either case, the writing came as a response to the destruction of the temple and to events leading up to and following that destruction.

From 66 to 70 CE a Jewish revolt broke out against Rome. This revolt was incited by the raiding of the temple treasury by the procurator Gessius Florus. In 67 Emperor Nero placed responsibility for stilling the uprising in the hands of his veteran general, Vespasian.[2] Vespasian conquered territories of Palestine, working his way to Jerusalem until 68 when Nero died, after which Vespasian assumed the seat as emperor (one year later) and left his son, Titus, to command the armies. In 70 CE Titus marched Roman troops into Jerusalem, where he encountered intense resistance from diverse but united Jewish factions. The temple, which had recently undergone extravagant renovation, was burned, bringing to an end the second temple period.

Although Jerusalem was destroyed and the temple burned two years after the death of Nero, he became the focus of much anti-Roman rhetoric, because it was he who began the campaign against Jerusalem that ended in the destruction of the temple. Nero was also known for his persecution of Christians and Jews (keep in mind that Christianity was considered a sect of Judaism up to the fourth century) in his home city of Rome. In 64 a disastrous fire had broken out in Rome, and the rumor persisted that Nero, having started the fire to clear the area for his building campaigns, had diverted attention from himself by accusing his "dissenters," which included Christians, of the crime. The rumor holds that those arrested were afflicted with cruel punishments, such as being burned to death in one of Nero's gardens, and so severe were the punishments that the surrounding population began to doubt the Christians' guilt. It is possible that the apostles Peter and Paul were put to death in this persecution.[3]

Regardless of whether Nero accused Christians of burning Rome, it is a fact that he and the Roman emperor Domitian persecuted them. These two rulers each proclaimed they were deity and demanded that the people address them as "Lord and God." Rome thus became known as the city of God. However, participation in imperial worship, which was integrated into Roman culture with public events such as sacrifices to the emperor, was impossible for faithful Jews and Christians, so they were viewed as bad citizens, subversives, and a threat that needed to be eliminated. While the Roman Empire was known for its peaceful existence, or *Pax Romana*, this "peace" was kept through military might. There was very little tolerance for difference or rebellious activity, and so groups like the Christians and the Jews who worshiped their own God exclusively and refused to participate in the imperial cult were certain to be persecuted. This persecution was sporadic, localized, and enforced at the whim of capricious emperors rather than constant, widespread, and systematic. This hostile, oppressive, and uncertain environment provides the sociopolitical context for understanding the writing of John of Patmos.

John envisions an impending increase in persecution due to escalating conflicts between Christians and the Roman Empire over their abstinence from idolatry of any sort. Consequently, John writes to provide encouragement and comfort. The encouragement is a call to remain faithful, even to the point of death, in worship and in testimony to God and to Jesus the Messiah. The hope lies in a longed-for appearance of Jesus, during which faithful Christians would be gathered, martyrs would receive their reward, and all that is evil would be judged and conquered. John communicates his apocalypse of encouragement and hope through an elaborate narrative of visions told through symbolic characters and events (see the outline below).

Key Characters and Events
Given the length and complexity of Revelation, it is impossible to discuss the entire book in one chapter. However, an interpretation of the key characters and events will be helpful for understanding the critique of the Left Behind perspective that comes in the following chapters. For many of us the mere mention of the book of Revelation conjures up images of devils, beasts, and monsters with many heads, but surprisingly the majority of characters and events in John's apocalypse are positive. In fact, these outnumber the negative characters and events almost two to one. These include: the seven churches (chaps. 1–3), God (chaps. 4, 21), the twenty-four elders (chaps. 4, 5, 7, 11, 14, 19), the 144,000 (chaps. 7, 14), the two witnesses (chap. 11), the woman clothed with the sun and her

Outline of Revelation
Introductory material (1:1-8)

Inaugural vision of Jesus Christ among the churches and messages to the seven churches (1:9–3:22)

Inaugural vision of heaven (4:1–5:14)

Seven seals (6:1–8:5)

Seven trumpets (8:6–11:19)

Story of God's people in conflict with evil (12:1–15:4)

Seven bowls (15:5–16:21)

Babylon the harlot (17:1–19:10)

Destruction of Babylon and the new Jerusalem (19:11–21:8)

New Jerusalem as the bride of Christ (21:9–22:9)

Epilogue (22:10-21)

child (chap. 12), the Lamb (chap. 5, 14), martyrs (chaps. 6, 20), Michael and the good angels (chap. 12), the rider from heaven (chap. 19), the establishment of a new heaven and the new earth (chap. 21), and the appearance of a new Jerusalem (chaps. 21–22). Some of these are very easy to identify. God is God, of course, and the seven churches of John's inaugural vision, to whom he addresses letters of affirmation and/or condemnation (1:9–3:22), are actual known historic locations. Other images are far more complex, so it is important to spend some time exploring them.

Many readers may have grown up, as I did, hearing about the **144,000** who would be saved in the end. I remember thinking it was really unfair that only 144,000 people would be saved but secretly hoping I was one of them. This number ought not to be taken literally, though. The number is depicted as 12,000 people from each of the twelve tribes of Israel (Revelation 7:5-8). In fact, John interprets the 144,000 for us: "there was a great multitude that no one could count, from every nation, from all tribes and peoples and languages" (7:9). The 144,000 are symbolic of a group so large that nobody can count it, and the group is made up of people from every nation. The image is a symbol of completeness and inclusion—not one of the redeemed will be missing.

The 144,000 appear standing with the Lamb on Mount Zion, each marked with the seal of God (Revelation 14:1 in contrast to the mark of the Beast in v. 9). They are said to be virgins, never having defiled themselves with a woman. Some have taken this literally and suggested the 144,000 are all male virgins. However, when reading Revelation, which is filled with metaphoric language, we ought to think symbolically. Just as some of the aforementioned seven churches are charged with fornication, which is a metaphor for idolatry, the 144,000 are said to be virgins, which is a metaphor for those who remained faithful to God and stayed away from the pagan cults. Female sexual imagery is often used in the Bible to describe the people's faithfulness or unfaithfulness. The prophets,

THE FACTS BEHIND THE FICTION

for example, frequently accuse Israel of harlotry because the people incorporated worship of Canaanite gods into their worship, and on occasion Israel is referred to as God's virgin daughter (Lamentations 1:15; 2:13), an image intended to emphasize innocence and conjure up empathy for Israel. Based on this common usage, John's image of 144,000 virgins makes most sense if understood as a reference to those who have never engaged in foreign worship.

The **two witnesses** represent the whole church in their role as prophetic witness to the world. There are two because, according to the Law of Moses, adequate testimony requires two witnesses (Deuteronomy 19:15). The two witnesses are modeled after Moses and Elijah, both of whom confronted idolatry in their day. They are seen wearing sackcloth, which signals that they bear a message of repentance. We are reminded here again of the message to the seven churches in which each church was affirmed for any faithful acts, exhorted to refrain from idolatry, and called to proclaim that same message to the Roman Empire.

The **woman clothed with the sun** with the moon under her feet is first portrayed in labor, then giving birth to a Child who is to shepherd all the nations with a rod of iron (Revelation 12:5). The Child is snatched away and taken to God and to his throne (12:6). It is impossible to read this text and not think of Mary giving birth to Jesus; thus it is an allusion. At the same time, though, the woman appears to be the heavenly representative of God's people, first as Israel from whom Jesus the Messiah was born (12:5) and then as the Christian church persecuted by the Dragon (12:13). Revelation 11:1-2 tells of John being advised to measure the temple (but not the outer court) as a means of protecting the inner being of the church even though it may be martyred. Similarly, Revelation 12:14 depicts the spiritual protection of the church during conflict with the Dragon and the Beast. The woman is all at once less and more of each of these allusions. In John's artistry, he conflates several images into one new image. The image of the woman pulls together elements from the pagan myth of the Queen of Heaven; from the Genesis story of Eve; from the traditions around Israel's escape from the dragon pharaoh into the wilderness on the wings of an eagle (Exodus 19:4; Psalm 74:12-15); and from Zion, the mother of the people of God from whom the Messiah comes (Isaiah 66:7-19).

The **Child** is Jesus the Messiah, who is most often depicted in Revelation as the **Lamb**. As the Lamb, Jesus stands in sharp contrast to the military image in 19:11, where he appears on a white horse to judge and make war. It is the work of the Lamb that has won the real victory, for he has brought redemption to the world through his blood. The military Jesus simply comes to sweep up the mess at the end, after which, the **martyrs,** those who have been slaughtered for their testimony and who are depicted as crying "How long?" under the altar (6:9-10), come to life to reign with Christ.

Finally, the **new heaven,** the **new earth,** and the **new Jerusalem** appear. Little is said about the new heaven and the new earth (Revelation 21:1), but the new Jerusalem is described as the bride of the Lamb filled with the glory of God. She has the radiance of a rare jewel and a great high wall with twelve gates that are named after the twelve tribes of Israel. The wall of the new city sits on twelve foundations that are named after the twelve apostles of the Lamb. Running through the middle of the city is the river of the water of life that flows forth from the throne of God and of the Lamb; and on either side of the river stands the tree of life, which bears twelve kinds of fruit and healing leaves (22:2). The twelve twelves of the tribes and the apostles represent the blending of Israel and the church, as do the 144,000, which include 12,000 people from the twelve tribes as well as the **twenty-four elders.** The elders represent leaders drawn from the twelve tribes along with the twelve apostles. They sit on thrones around the throne of God, and all are equal participants in what will take place in the consummation of history.

THE FACTS BEHIND THE FICTION

While the negative images of Revelation are fewer in number, they are memorable. They include the Dragon (chap. 12), the beast from the sea (chaps. 12-13), the beast from the land (chap. 13), the harlot and Babylon (chaps. 17–18), bad angels (chaps. 9, 12), the dead (chap. 20), and Hades and the lake of fire (chaps. 1, 6, 19, 20). The **Dragon**, also called the devil and Satan, is identified for readers in 12:9, where John once again draws on Genesis 3:15, which depicts the age-long conflict between "the ancient serpent" and the woman's seed. This image is conflated with the image of Leviathan the sea monster or dragon. Leviathan is presented in Isaiah 27:1 as destined for ultimate defeat by the sword of God and in Psalm 74:13-14 (and writings outside the Bible) as a dragon with seven heads. By fusing the serpent of Genesis with Leviathan, John has created an ultimate image of evil. The seven crowns (for the seven heads) represent the fullness of power behind all idolatrous human rule (Daniel 8:10). The Dragon's heads and horns challenge the Lamb's horns (Revelation 5:6), and with the flick of his tale, the Dragon sends a third of the stars falling from heaven. This scenario represents the Dragon's infliction of suffering on the people of God on earth.

When the woman clothed with the sun was about to bear her Son, the Dragon stood ready to devour the Child before the Child was snatched away to his heavenly throne. Then **Michael and his angels** fought against the dragon and threw him and his **(bad) angels** down to earth. Once confined to earth, the Dragon raises a **beast from the sea** to which he delegates his remaining powers (13:1-2). This beast image is a conflation into one of the four beasts found in Daniel 7, and it represents the Roman Empire and its emperors.[4] The number seven suggests totality, and this beast has seven heads, equal to the sum of all the heads on Daniel's beasts and representative of a series of Roman emperors alluded to in 17:9. Thus the Beast represents the totality of human rule as evidenced in the empire that ruled the writer's and reader's known world—Rome, the ultimate beastly world power.

Although it is difficult to determine which seven emperors John has in mind, Nero certainly is one and Domitian is probably another. The idea here is that the eighth ruler will be the Son of Man as depicted in Revelation 14:14, who will come to displace the Roman Empire with the kingdom of God. The ten horns of the Beast are a derivative of Daniel's fourth beast, and John gives them crowns to emphasize their kingly nature. The blasphemous names written on their heads reflect the divine titles, such as "Son of God" and "Lord and God," that were taken by some of the emperors. The Beast is said to suffer a mortal wound to one of its heads, but the wound is healed (13:3). This wounding likely represents the death of Nero, after which the Roman Empire suffered a one-year period of anarchy that was remedied by Vespasian.

Some understand this reference as a parody of the death and resurrection of Jesus and others as a parody of the prophetic witness of the church as symbolized by the two witnesses. Similarly, the question of the people found at the close of 13:4, "Who is like the beast, and who can fight against it?" is understood as a parody of expressions of the uniqueness of God found in the Old Testament (e.g., Exodus 15:11; Isaiah 40:25). Revelation 13:5-10 emphasizes the temporary power the Beast has against the human race by calling the saints to endurance and faith during the time of persecution.

After the beast from the sea, John sees the rise of the **beast of the land**, which is called "the false prophet" (Revelation 16:13; 19:20; 20:10). This beast represents the priesthood of the imperial cult. The beast of the land performs miracles and deceives humans into making an image of the beast and receiving his mark, which allows them to participate in economic enterprises. Receiving the mark of the Beast is a parody of the protective seal given to faithful Christians by God in 7:3 and 14:1.

Much has been made over the years of the mark of the Beast, the **Antichrist**, and the number 666. I remember that when I was in college, an itinerate preacher proclaimed that Henry Kissinger was the Antichrist and that we all had his mark—our social security numbers. I suspect most readers can tell similar stories. While this is an example of the misapplication of a biblical image to contemporary times, Revelation 13 provides a clue to the identity of the beast from the sea by stating that the number of the Beast is also the number of a person. In Hebrew and Greek each letter of the alphabet also represents a number, so it is possible to add up the numbers represented by the letters of a person's name to identify him or her numerically. The emperor Nero's name, which would have been written as Nero(n) Caesar, adds up to 666.

Through the use of symbols and numbers, the author of Revelation is describing something that he and the first hearers experienced and were continuing to experience—persecution. John's focus is on Nero, who was known for violent persecution of Christians and Jews. For John, the Beast was the Roman Empire and the head that was wounded was the former emperor of Rome, Nero. Those who did not have the mark of the Beast, that is, anyone who had not received a voucher for offering sacrifices to the Roman gods and/or to the emperor, were frequently prohibited from buying and selling in Rome. The hope that John offered was that the end of this terrible time was near.

In chapter 17, Revelation introduces a woman sitting on a scarlet beast. The beast has the typical seven heads and ten horns, but it is unique in that it is scarlet, which most likely represents blood, as the woman is said to be intoxicated with the blood of witnesses to Jesus (v. 6). The woman, clothed in purple and adorned with precious metals and jewels, is holding a gold cup full of abominations. Her name as written on her forehead is "Babylon the great, mother of whores and of earth's abominations" (v. 6).

While the prophets often use the imagery of harlotry and adultery in the Old Testament to refer to Israel's unfaithfulness to God, that usage is only meaningful for God's people. Here the **harlot** imagery reflects the use found in Isaiah 23 where prostitution represents

Tyre's trading relationships with the nations. The beast on which she rides represents the military and political power of Rome, which makes possible the economic prosperity due to the commitments to *Pax Romana*. The only ones who benefit from this arrangement are the Roman elite and the "kings of the earth" from Revelation 17:2 who have committed fornication with the harlot. Most of the common people who are being exploited by the empire are so dazzled by the glory of Rome and her propaganda—"intoxicated with the wine of her adulteries," as 17:2b (NIV) puts it—that they do not recognize the exploitation. Babylon, the mother of whores, is Rome, the metropolis to which other urban centers, including those in which the seven churches are located, are subject. She is female because she is a holistic character representing the goddess *Roma* of the imperial cult as well as the political and economic facets of the city.

The vision of John provides an interpretation of the harlot and the beast on which she sits that further associates it with Nero. "But the angel said to me, 'Why are you so amazed? I will tell you the mystery of the woman, and of the beast with seven heads and ten horns that carries her. The beast that you saw was, and, is not, and is about to ascend from the bottomless pit and go to destruction'" (Revelation 17:7-8). This description reflects a popular myth of the day that Nero was not actually dead but had fled to the east and would return (or in some versions, was dead and would rise again), with allies to wreak havoc on Rome.[5] Playing on this myth, John creates a parody of Jesus' death, resurrection, and expected return by suggesting that those whose names are not in the Book of Life will be deceived by Nero's return into believing that he is the messiah.

The vision continues with an explanation that leaves no doubt that the entire image is about Rome. The seven heads of the beast are interpreted in the text (Revelation 17:9) as representing seven hills, for which Rome was famous. The heads are also interpreted as a line of seven kings who will "go to destruction" (vv. 9-11).

Included among those seven is the "beast that was and is not" (Nero, v. 11), even though he is falsely counted as the eighth, or ultimate, ruler. The Beast and his allies, who are represented by the ten horns on the seven heads of the Beast, will go to war against the true, ultimate ruler, the Lamb (vv. 12-14). The Lamb will conquer those who wage war against him. Once defeated, "**Babylon,**" which means Rome, will fall. Chapter 18 contains a dirge over that fallen city. In the end, after a final judgment, this world power will be replaced by a new Jerusalem (21:2).

John envisions a great reversal in the end. The Beast and the False Prophet are defeated, "thrown alive into the lake of fire" (Revelation 19:20), an image that represents a complete defeat. In contrast, the martyrs, those who were put to death by the Beast and the False Prophet, come back to life to reign with Christ in the new kingdom (20:4). The idea of the millennium is borrowed from the idea of a temporary period of messianic rule on earth before the renewal of creation found in Jewish writings contemporary to Revelation. The one thousand years need not be taken literally, as is the case with many numbers and times in Revelation, but represents a very long time, a time of vindication for those who have died for the faith.

Meanwhile, Satan, the ultimate principle of evil, has been bound for the duration of the new rule. But the reversal is not yet complete—not until Satan has his last opportunity to deceive the nations (20:7-8). Satan gathers the nations to battle against the saints and the beloved city (20:9); the armies are destroyed by fire from heaven, and Satan is thrown into the lake of fire, were he, the Beast, and the False Prophet will be tormented forever. In 20:13 Hades, Death, and the sea (apparently holding stations for the dead until God is ready for them) give up their dead for the final judgment. All who are associated with evil are sent to the lake of fire (the permanent abode for the dead). The focus here is not upon the individual judgment as much as the removal of evil. The reversal is complete, evil has been swept away, and good has prevailed. The environ is now prepared for the descent of the long-hoped-for new Jerusalem (see Isaiah 65:17-20)—the place where no tear will be shed, no pain will be felt, and no death will be experienced, for God will dwell there with the redeemed (Revelation 21:1-4). The imagery provides a vivid expression of the age-old eschatological hope for a society where the rules of heaven are at play, a society filled with equity and justice for all.

Summary
While the characters John describes are fascinating and lend them-selves to a solid story about good versus evil, the important ques-tion is "What does it all mean?" Fundamentally, the book is a word of encouragement for Christians to endure persecution as they witness to their faith in Jesus as the Messiah. Readers will see in chapter 6 that this statement challenges foundational pieces of Darbyite, futuristic, pretribulationist, premillennial dispensational-ism, which claims a seven-year tribulation of proportions never yet seen, rather than persecution in general, and insists that true believ-ers will not have to endure it.

Specifically, the apocalypse of John issued a call to Christians for nonviolent resistance to Rome's forced enculturation into the polit-ical, religious, social, and economic mandates of the empire. Similarly, we are called to resist the enculturation of our own day. The real battle is symbolically represented by the Child born of the woman dressed with the sun who is taken to heaven to defeat the Dragon. That imagery depicts the victory of Jesus, who through resistance to evil to the point of his own death, overcame it. Revelation calls the Christian community to do the same with the message that evil is overcome only through nonviolent resistance. Simply by choosing not to participate in evil, the faithful render it powerless. This nonviolent resistance ought not to be confused with passive behavior. There is nothing passive about it. The call, as evidenced by the image of the two witnesses in Revelation 11:1-3, is to refrain from evil while testifying to faith in Jesus as Messiah. It is a call to avoid all idolatry and to proclaim the gospel of Jesus the Christ.

Further, the message of John to the Christian community is to wait for Jesus, in whom there will be judgment and new creation. It is important to note that the faithful suffering of the Christian community is what ushers in the realization of the new heaven and the new earth, imagery that represents the new social order that has been hoped for since the time of the writing of Isaiah 65:17 and 66:22.

Finally, many have commented on the violence depicted in Revelation. It is important to keep in mind the symbolic and emphatic language of apocalypse. Additionally, in Revelation 19:11, the rider on the white horse is said to come in *righteousness* to judge and make war. This is the only figure in the book that is acknowledged in this manner. It is the work of the Lamb that has won the real victory, for he has brought redemption to the world through his own blood. It is the Lamb's act of nonviolent resistance that has broken the stronghold of sin and evil. The Dragon and the Beast make war on the saints, but their activity is clearly presented as evil. In contrast, Jesus' appearing is for the purpose of destroying all that is evil, eliminating injustice, and establishing the kingdom, which will be a new and just social order. Yet this happens only as the result of the witness of those who endure suffering for their faithfulness. In the end, if John's apocalypse teaches us anything, it is that the power through which God ushers in the kingdom is the same power that was revealed in the cross—the power of suffering love.

CHAPTER 6

Before the Tribulation Begins

Next to salvation, prophecy is the most exciting subject in the Bible! It answers all the major questions of life. Once you understand Bible prophecy and its difficult issues, you can look confidently to the future knowing God is in control even though the world seems out of control.

—Tim LaHaye,
Left Behind Video Study Series brochure

In the development of the premillennial dispensational system, John Darby introduced an end-times schema that rests on the two core interpretive principles. These principles are a dichotomy between Israel and the church and a literal interpretation of the Bible, which results in the juxtaposition of isolated verses taken from a variety of biblical books. Essentially, what Darby did almost two hundred years ago was create a doctrine that necessitated Jesus come again, not once, but twice—first to rapture the church and a second time to establish his kingdom and millennial reign on earth.

Never before in the history of the church had such doctrines been held. Traditional Christian theology has always looked for Jesus Christ to put an end to inequity and injustice, to judge the wicked and save the righteous, and to create a new world order in which equity and justice will rule. But Darby and those who have followed his teaching have added significant details to this accepted understanding. By suggesting that God's interaction with people, past, present, and future, is divided into distinct time periods that are characterized by different tests of human obedience, dispensationalists have created a reality in which God treats people from different eras in different ways.

The tremendous success of the Left Behind series, which is grounded in a Darbyite, futuristic, pretribulationist, premillennial dispensationalism, has prompted Tim LaHaye to start a Left Behind certificate program. For several hundred dollars, an individual can enroll in this program that will lead him or her through five study units, each with six video-taped lectures by LaHaye and other "prophecy teachers." These study units, according to the brochure, will teach individuals how to interpret Bible prophecy for themselves so they can find answers to all the major questions of life. That's quite a claim! But can it be sustained?

Answering this question depends on examining key end-time events and the scriptural calisthenics needed to support them. In this chapter, we will look at events and phenomena that the authors claim will unfold prior to the period they call "the Tribulation." Many of the ideas presented in this chapter are camouflaged in the Left Behind series. This is partly due to the fact that the series is fiction rather than a systematic presentation of premillennial dispensationalism doctrines. Also the emphasis of the story line, and the focus of chapter 7 of this book, is on those who have been left behind to suffer the tribulation following removal of the true church. Thus, the categorization of believers, pretribulational and tribulational, is not readily evident in the series. The focus of this chapter is the identification of key characters and events from the novels as well as an explanation of particular beliefs that are played out in parts of the story line.

According to LaHaye and Jenkins, the rapture does not actually mark the beginning of the tribulation; rather, this great period of trial is initiated by a treaty the Antichrist signs with Israel. (Readers may want to revisit the table on page 5.) The events and phenomena that must be in place before the tribulation can begin are the apostasy of the church; the blooming in the desert, which leads to a sneak attack from the north; the building of a third temple; the rebuilding of Babylon; the rapture of true believers; and the signing of the treaty. The Scripture passages used to build this pretribulation scenario are taken from twenty-one different Bible passages found in twelve different biblical books, eight New Testament and four Old Testament.

The Great Apostasy

The emphasis on apostasy is not surprising since the Christian church has struggled for centuries with the idea of who is in and who is out, with questions of who holds and who does not hold "orthodox" (accepted) theology, and with the issue of which biblical interpretation is correct. Some have killed for their stances, while others have been martyred or have simply been excommunicated by the church. Premillennial dispensationalists anticipate a great apostasy, the roots of which are visible in the apostasy of contemporary America, in which the church has supposedly fallen away from the true faith.

The Left Behind novels have a character named Peter Mathews who rejects fundamental Christian doctrine and eventually becomes the leader of the apostate one-world religion. Peter, however, is not entirely fiction. He is representative of church leaders like Episcopal bishop John Shelby Spong, who in the words of LaHaye and Jenkins, "enthusiastically promotes . . . heretical views."[1] According to LaHaye and Jenkins, true believers are obedient to the "plain teaching of Scripture" and supportive of conservative government policies. They are members of growing, dynamic congregations that "teach the Bible, depend upon the ministry of the Holy Spirit, and do the work of evangelism," and who have saved the *nation* of America from becoming totally secularized.[2]

Conversely, the apostate churches are mainline denominations, such as Presbyterians and Methodists, that were infected by apostate ministers who had been indoctrinated in apostate seminaries, (Union Theological Seminary and the like) who join with pro-communist organizations to focus on liberal social causes while viciously attacking moral absolutes. According to LaHaye and Jenkins, God gave up these apostates to their "reprobate minds" but overruled the apostasy of the twentieth century through people like D. L. Moody and the establishment of Bible institutes, Christian colleges, and training centers.[3] In other words, churches that retain an ethic of social justice—that is, believe the Bible teaches Christians to strive for justice and equity for all people—are apostate because they do not hold to the "moral absolutes" promoted by those who share the view of LaHaye and Jenkins.

While the great apostasy climaxes after the rapture and during the tribulation when "conditions will be ripe for . . . those who call themselves Christians but are not really such, to turn their backs on God,"[4] apostate tendencies are evident before the rapture. The apostasy of today's mainline churches along with their decline in membership is identified by LaHaye and Jenkins as one of the many signs that we are in the end times.[5]

LaHaye and Jenkins's analysis of the church's drift toward apostasy is based primarily on four Bible verses: Three of these speak about a time when people will pervert (Jude 1:4), rebel against (2 Thessalonians 2:1-3), or depart from the faith (1 Timothy 4:1-2). And the fourth is taken from the letter to the church in Laodicea, which was evaluated as being neither hot nor cold (Revelation 3:15). According to the authors, there are two camps, premillennial dispensationalism and the remainder of Christendom, which is essentially apostate (forsaking their true faith). While these verses provide real warnings about people leaving the faith, they do not provide a systematic presentation of what the doctrines of the faith ought to include. LaHaye and Jenkins don't explain their case in these terms either. They simply assume their interpretation is correct and everyone else is apostate, even though major portions of the Christian world disagree with them.

Blooming in the Desert and a Disastrous Sneak Attack from the North

While LaHaye and Jenkins claim that most of the major events depicted in their Left Behind series are based directly on specific biblical prophecies, they state they have invented "imaginative elements" to move the plot along. One of these inventions is a secret chemical compound developed by Israeli scientist Chaim Rosenzweig that makes the desert bloom and its inventors rich. This literary device was created to support two plot lines that, according to the authors, are grounded in biblical prophecy: These are the extraordinary blessing of God on the physical land of Israel and a surprise attack by Russia and its allies against Israel.[6] According to the story as it is told in volume 1, *Left Behind*, Chaim Rosenzweig's invention causes every inch of ground in Israel to blossom with flowers and grains as never before, resulting in the Holy Land becoming the export capital of the world. Thus everyone in Israel becomes very prosperous and the rest of the world grows envious.

This prosperity leads to a surprise attack on Israel by envious Russia, whose economy is devastated and technology regressing. The attack, as described in the book and dramatized in the *Left Behind* movie, involves all of Russia's military air power, yet miraculously no one in Israel is killed. The Russian fleet is completely devastated, but the planes crash in open areas, thus sparing all the buildings and all human life in Israel. The only people who die are the Russian pilots. In contrast, Israel is able to gather combustible material from the wreckage that will serve as fuel and preserve their natural resources for more than six years.

This opening scene of the Left Behind series, according to LaHaye and Jenkins, depicts the realization of unfulfilled biblical prophecy. The first of these is God's promise to Israel that its desert land will be turned into a lush garden (Isaiah 35:1-2, 6-7; 41:18-20; and 43:19). While LaHaye and Jenkins believe this prediction will be fulfilled during Jesus' millennial kingdom on earth, they see the blossoming of flowers and grains in the desert as preparation for that event.[7]

The attack by Russia is intended to depict the fulfillment of Ezekiel 38:1-2, which reads, "The word of the LORD came to me: 'Son of man, set your face against Gog, of the land of Magog, the chief prince of Meshech and Tubal; prophesy against him and say, 'This is what the Sovereign LORD says: I am against you, O Gog, chief prince of Meshech and Tubal'" (NIV). LaHaye and Jenkins quote an earlier work by LaHaye as evidence that "etymologically" Gog and Magog can only mean modern-day Russia, because "Magog was the second son of Japheth, who according to Josephus the great historian, settled north of the Black Sea."[8] The authors assert that this is reaffirmed by the references in Ezekiel 38:15 and 39:2 to the attacking nation coming from the far north, saying, "All Bible directions are given in relation to Israel. . . . 'south' means south of Israel, etc. Any map will show that Russia is indeed north of Israel."[9]

Also mentioned in Ezekiel 38–39 are Gog's allies, Persia, Ethiopia, Libya, Gomer, and Togarmah. According to LaHaye and Jenkins, these countries are all contemporary Arab Muslim countries, and they "'just happen'" to be allied with Russia and have a "binding, overriding, passionate, and common hatred" for Israel. They also note that 55 million of Russia's 250 million people are Arabs, "most of whom hate Israel."[10] Thus, they conclude, the end times will see an attack on Israel by Arab Muslim countries through Russia.

There are many problems with these conclusions—problems that stem from a reading of biblical texts with very little thought given to the chronology and historicity of events. In other words, it is a forced fit. LaHaye and Jenkins say the three Isaiah texts refer to a time yet to come when Jesus will return to reign in Jerusalem for a millennium, suggesting that these texts are unfulfilled prediction. Yet the verses around these texts make it clear that each addresses Israel's return to Jerusalem after the Babylonian exile. They are poetic depictions of the desert's response to Israel's return to her beloved land, which actually took place nearly five hundred years before the birth of Jesus.

In Ezekiel, Gog is referred to as a leader of an invading army from the far north that will attack the people of Israel in the latter years. Chapters 33–39 record God's promise of restoration after the exile. The triumph of God over the ultimate enemy, Gog, described in chapters 38–39, paves the way for God's reenthronement (Ezekiel 40–48). The defeat of Gog serves as vindication of God's holiness and a demonstration of God's might while proving that the nation's sinfulness, not God's weakness or lack of concern, led Israel into exile. These were extremely important theological concepts because the surrounding nations believed in many gods that were attached to geographical locations, in particular to cities. Consequently, when Jerusalem was destroyed by Babylon, Jerusalem's neighbors would have understood that Babylon's gods were more powerful and worthier of worship, but the return vindicates the God of Israel as the one true God. The author of Revelation borrows the Gog and Magog imagery to describe the final assault against God's people and the beloved city (Revelation 20:8-9). This is not unusual, as Gog and Magog are also found in other writings from this period.

The identification of Magog is uncertain at best. In Ezekiel, Gog is a person and Magog a territory, while in Revelation both Gog and Magog are used as names of evil nations. The claim by LaHaye and Jenkins that the great historian Josephus understood Magog to be the second son of Japheth (who was the third son of

Noah), who settled north of the Black Sea, is slightly off the point. Josephus understood Magog to refer to the Scythians.[11] He also may have believed that the second son of Japheth settled north of the Black Sea, and he even may have believed the descendants of Japheth evolved into the Scythians, but this line of descent certainly is not straight, and it does not lead to modern-day Russia. Additionally, Josephus's conclusions have nothing to do with the study of derivation (etymology) of the word *Magog*. The word may have originally meant "land of Gyges," or it may simply reflect the Hebrew *ma*, which means "place of," with Magog meaning "place of Gog." In the Aramaic translation of the Hebrew Bible, the name is interpreted as *Germania*, and the fourth-century church father Jerome understood Magog to refer to the Goths.

A Third Temple

LaHaye and Jenkins see in our contemporary age signs that the temple in Jerusalem will be rebuilt.[12] While they are not certain whether the temple will be built a third time before or shortly after the tribulation begins, they assert that the rebuilding is unquestionably predicted in Scripture and that the temple needs to be complete and operational by the middle of the seven-year tribulation. The reconstruction of the temple is celebrated as a great day for Israel in volume two of the fiction series (*Tribulation Force*) as it also displaces the current Moslem mosque that sits on the temple site and defiles that holy place. Support for the belief in a third temple begins with the authors' identification of several references to a desolation of the temple found in the book of Daniel (9:27; 11:31), on the lips of Jesus (Matthew 24:15), in the writings of Paul (2 Thessalonians 2:3-4), and in Revelation 11:1-2, which reads: "Then I was given a measuring rod like a staff, and I was told, "'Come and measure the temple of God and the altar and those who worship there, but do not measure the court outside the temple; leave that out, for it is given over to the nations, and they will trample over the holy city for forty-two months.'"

The authors conclude that the temple must be rebuilt so that this "prophecy" of a great desolation can be fulfilled. However, nowhere in the book of Revelation, nor anywhere else in the Bible, is it stated that the temple will be rebuilt. LaHaye and Jenkins have drawn their conclusion about a third temple strictly from deductive reasoning based on unrelated texts, without giving credence to historical context or genre of those texts. The references in Daniel, Matthew, and 2 Thessalonians refer to historical events related to the desecration of the second temple, first by Antiochus Epiphanes IV in 167 BCE, then in 70 CE when it was destroyed by the Romans. Therefore, these verses are irrelevant to the argument that a third temple must be built. The book of Revelation was written after the destruction of the second temple, yet the vision of Revelation 11 calls John of Patmos to measure the temple, the altar, and those who worship there. This then is the only text that needs our attention.

Revelation is a self-designated apocalypse (Revelation 1:1) and as such is filled with symbolic imagery, which explains why the writer of the book could be called to "measure" a nonexistent temple. The reference is metaphorical. Later in the book (chaps. 21–22), it is actually proclaimed that there will not be a temple in the new Jerusalem, but rather God will make a dwelling in the community of the redeemed saints. For the writer of Revelation, the temple is not a literal building, but the Christian community that worships God.[13] This idea was already present in Paul's thought, which informed the theology of John and his faith community. For example 1 Corinthians 3:16 reads, "Do you not know that you are God's temple and that God's Spirit dwells in you?" The measuring of the temple in Revelation 11:2 ought, then, to be understood as marking the faith community for protection, the equivalent to the sealing of the church as found in Revelation 7:1-8, which promises that those who have been marked (or sealed) will be stamped as God's own even if they experience suffering and death.

The Rebuilding of Babylon

The rebuilding of the temple is not the only anticipated rebuilding that LaHaye and Jenkins see beginning to take shape. They believe Babylon must be rebuilt because it is predicted in Scripture to be the city from which the Antichrist reigns during the tribulation. The reasons for this interpretation are twofold: first, Babylon is mentioned numerous times in the book of Revelation, and second, several "prophecies" about Babylon's destruction have not yet been fulfilled.[14] Since Babylon's destruction is predicted two times each in Isaiah (chaps. 13 and 14) and Jeremiah (chaps. 50 and 51), the authors conclude that fulfillment requires two destructions. The first destruction took place in 539 BCE with the Persian conquest that resulted in the Jews returning to their homeland. The second destruction necessitates a rebuilt Babylon. Additionally, they turn to Isaiah 21:9 and Revelation 14:8 and 18:2. LaHaye and Jenkins come to their conclusions based on an "ancient rabbinic rule" of interpretation that says when the Bible mentions an event twice, it means the event will happen twice.[15] Each of these texts begins with the phrase "Babylon is fallen, fallen." So, according to their rule, since the "fallen" is used twice, Babylon must fall twice; and in order to fall a second time, it must be rebuilt. Further, the authors conclude that Jeremiah 51:8, 26; Isaiah 13:19; and Revelation 18 clearly state that Babylon will be suddenly and totally destroyed and the ruins will never again be inhabited. However, other cities have been built on the site, and the city was not destroyed completely as predicted; therefore, it must be rebuilt so that these predictions can come to pass.[16]

All of the biblical texts cited in support of the notion of a rebuilt Babylon come from Jeremiah, Isaiah, and Revelation. These books are filled with poetry and imagery. The people yearned for the day of Babylon's destruction, and they spoke about it in emphatic ways. Two of the predominant literary conventions apparent throughout the Old Testament are repetition and hyperbole. Repetition in Hebrew creates emphasis, so the phrase "Babylon is fallen, fallen" emphasizes the destruction of the city. Similarly, when Jeremiah and Isaiah spoke of the utter destruction of Babylon, they depicted a thorough destruction in hyperbolic fashion as a means of emphasizing their intense relief and satisfaction concerning this event.

As we explored in chapter 5, the book of Revelation reflects a particular set of historical circumstances. The book was probably written around 90 CE. Jewish and Christian literature written after the destruction of Jerusalem in 70 CE frequently used Babylon as a transparent metaphor for Rome because Rome had destroyed Jerusalem and the temple just as the Babylonians had done centuries before. The author of Revelation uses Babylon as a veil for Rome to magnify its sins and intensify negative feelings toward Rome among the first readers/hearers of the apocalypse. Revelation 17–18 predicts the fall of Rome, but LaHaye and Jenkins read the text as a literal reference to another destruction of Babylon and conclude it must be rebuilt. And they not only believe that it will be rebuilt—they believe it *has already been* rebuilt. They claim that the work begun in 1999 by Saddam Hussein (which has since ceased) was fulfillment of this prediction by a "demon-possessed" satanist who saw himself as a replacement for Nebuchadnezzar and believed his destiny was to rule the world.[17] The question that arises at this point is, why go to such lengths to support this notion of a rebuilt Babylon when it is not supported in the biblical text? The answer is that the notion is essential to the theological system within which LaHaye and Jenkins operate. A rebuilt Babylon provides the location from which the Antichrist will rule the world after he kicks off the tribulation by signing a treaty with Israel. But first, true believers must be snatched away from the impending terror.

The Rapture

As mentioned in chapter 2, Darby understood the distinction between "Jewish and Gentile dispensations" to be the "hinge" on which all interpretation of Scripture turns.[18] Specifically, he held that when a biblical text refers to Israel, the reader is to look for a plain and direct testimony because earthly things are Israel's proper portion. However, when the biblical text refers to Gentiles or the church, the reader should look for symbols because earthly things are not their portion. Reading the Bible in this manner, Darby concluded that the church was destined to share all things with Christ—all honor, glory, and majesty both in heaven and on earth. Israel, on the other hand, had its hope in the literal, earthly fulfillment of the covenant promised to it in the Old Testament. One implication of this core dispensational principle of an Israel-church dichotomy is the privileged status of the church.

In the dispensational view, the church has a peculiar character and special connection to Christ. According to Darby, the church was not in God's original plan but came into being only after Israel rejected Jesus as the Messiah. A remnant from Israel, who did accept Jesus as Messiah, was set aside to create the church as recorded in Acts 2, the day of Pentecost. That moment marked the end of the dispensation of law (Israel) and the beginning of the dispensation of grace (the Christian church). In this view, the church has since become corrupted beyond redemption by the imposition of human standards and administrations.[19] Repair of the ruins of the church are beyond human ability, and all efforts to do so are sinful.[20]

Darby made such bold statements because he believed the dispensation of the church would end when Christ comes to remove from earth this holy remnant, or "true church," which consists of those who have remained pure in the Holy Spirit by means of separating themselves from evil. In Darby's thought, the true church *is* the literal body of Christ and *already* sits with Christ in the heavenly places, so its hope lies, not in Christ's return to earth, but in its own ascension to its rightful place in heaven. The raptured church will go to the judgment seat of Christ, where it will be deemed righteous and then be ushered into the marriage supper of the Lamb as Christ's bride. Jesus will return to earth with his bride after a period of tribulation to rebuild the Jewish kingdom of heaven (dispensationalists distinguish this from the kingdom of God, which they consider the rule of God in the human heart) on earth. Israel will once again occupy the land, the temple will be rebuilt, and the sacrificial system will be reinstituted. Jesus will sit on the throne of David, and the nations of the world will acknowledge Israel as the favored people of God.

This rapture doctrine has sustained nearly two hundred years of use and has been given new life in the fiction of the Left Behind series. Revealing an interpretive process that involves weaving together Bible verses that are taken out of their larger contexts and reading the resultant created text through the lens of Darbyite, futuristic, pretribulationist, premillennial dispensational presuppositions, LaHaye and Jenkins outline the doctrine of rapture in *The Authorized Left Behind Handbook*.[21] They begin their discussion with 1 Thessalonians 4:13-18.

> But I would not have you to be ignorant, brethren, concerning them which are asleep, that ye sorrow not, even as others which have no hope. For if we believe that Jesus died and rose again, even so them also which sleep in Jesus will God bring with him. For this we say unto you by the word of the Lord, that we which are alive and remain unto the coming of the Lord shall not prevent them which are asleep. For the Lord himself shall descend from heaven with a shout, with the voice

of the archangel, and with the trump of God; and the dead in Christ shall rise first; Then we which are alive and remain shall be caught up together with them in the clouds, to meet the Lord in the air: and so shall we ever be with the Lord. Wherefore comfort one another with these words. (KJV)

The word translated "caught up" is crucial to making this the key biblical text for the concept of rapture. However, in order to fill out the doctrine, it is necessary to combine this verse with additional biblical texts. Next, the authors incorporate 1 Corinthians 15:51-54. From this passage they deduce that those being "caught up" with Christ are headed toward heaven.

Behold, I shew you a mystery; We shall not all sleep, but we shall all be changed. In a moment, in the twinkling of an eye, at the last trump: for the trumpet shall sound, and the dead shall be raised incorruptible, and we shall be changed. For this corruptible must put on incorruption, and this mortal [must] put on immortality. So when this corruptible shall have put on incorruption, and this mortal shall have put on immortality, then shall be brought to pass the saying that is written, Death is swallowed up in victory. (KJV)

LaHaye and Jenkins interpret "shall be changed" to mean "made incorruptible by having our bodies made 'immortal'"[22] and from this conclusion deduce that the destination of the caught-up believers is heaven with Jesus. To make this point clear, they insert phrases from 1 Corinthians 15:51-54 between phrases of 1 Thessalonians 4:17 to build their doctrine of the rapture: "Then we who are alive and remain {1 Thessalonians 4:17a} shall be changed (made incorruptible by having our bodies made 'immortal'; 1 Corinthians 15:51, 53). Then we shall be caught up [raptured] together (1 Thessalonians 4:17{b})."[23]

Next, the "mystery" introduced by Paul in 1 Corinthians 15:51-54 that "we shall all be changed, in a moment, in the twinkling of an eye," is further explained and exemplified with a shift to Genesis 5:24, "Enoch walked with God: then he was no more, because God took him away" (NIV). The authors claim "all believers will be transformed like the godly Enoch, whose earthly body was suddenly made fit to be in heaven with God."[24] Finally, to solidify their interpretation of the ultimate destination being heaven, they turn to John 14:2-3: "In my Father's house are many mansions: if it were not so, I would have told you. I go to prepare a place for you. And if I go and prepare a place for you, I will come again, and receive you unto myself; that where I am, there ye may be also" (KJV). Portions of these verses are inserted between the phrases in 1 Thessalonians 4:17 and rendered: "To meet the Lord in the air (1 Thessalonians 4:17). To 'receive you to Myself . . . {so} that {w}here I am, there you may be also' (John 14:3). 'And thus we shall always be with the Lord' (1 Thessalonians 4:17)."[25]

This use of Scripture to create the doctrine of rapture violates several of the principles for reading Scripture outlined in chapter 4. First, LaHaye and Jenkins draw isolated verses from several different biblical books, books written by different authors in different time periods, giving no attention to the meaning of these verses within their original context(s), and then braid them together. In doing this, they essentially create a new literary text and thus a new meaning. While some readers (not this author) might find this method of stringing texts together acceptable in this case due to their common themes, a close look at the verses raises significant concerns.

While the verses from 1 Thessalonians and 1 Corinthians deal with the resurrection of the dead and the return of the Lord, neither text mentions the final destination of the believers. In fact, some well-noted Pauline scholars have suggested the believers are meeting Christ in the air to usher him back to earth as his entourage, so to speak.[26] The conclusion that the true church is whisked away to heaven must be inferred through the preunderstanding that Israel and the church are distinct and that the true church has a privileged status that results in rescue prior to a coming tribulation period.[27] Such a conclusion requires interpreting these two biblical passages completely out of their contexts.

The context of 1 Corinthians 15 reveals that the entire chapter is crafted to counter doubts about the doctrine of the resurrection of the dead. Paul asks in verse 12, "How can some of you say there is no resurrection of the dead?" and then argues for acceptance of the doctrine of resurrection through reference to the resurrection of Jesus, "If Christ has not been raised, then our proclamation has been in vain and . . . we are even found to be misrepresenting God" (1 Corinthians 15:14-15). Having covered the issue of whether the resurrection actually occurred, he next addresses the question, "How are the dead raised?" with "We will not all die, but we will all be changed" (1 Corinthians 15:35, 51).

In 1 Thessalonians 4, Paul is writing for an entirely different purpose: to comfort the believers in Thessalonica with the hope that the dead will be resurrected and that both the living and the dead will be with the Lord forever. Paul says that he does not want the Thessalonians to be uninformed, so that they will not grieve as others do who have no hope (v. 13). While Paul's purpose is to provide a sense of hope, that hope is primarily based on the resurrection of those among the community of believers who have already died. His description of what will transpire when Jesus returns is limited to that one brief sentence in verse 17, "We who are alive, who are left, will be caught up in the clouds together with them to meet the Lord in the air; and so we will be with the Lord forever." Paul does not suggest where believers will live with the Lord forever; nor does he make a distinction between Israel and the church.

While the literary context is crucial for understanding these texts, so too is the broader context of Paul's overall thought about what will take place when Jesus returns. There is no indication in Paul's writings that he presumed different roles for Israel and the church; nor is there evidence that Paul envisioned the church going immediately to heaven. In fact, traditional scholarship in Pauline studies suggests that Paul's writings evidence a belief that Jesus would return to be with his people (one collective group) on earth.

John 14:2-3 does suggest that Jesus has returned to his Father's house to prepare a place for his followers and that he will come again to take them unto himself; however, it says nothing about resurrection or rapture. Here we bump into the premillennial dispensational core principle of "literal interpretation." Is the image of the Father's house with many rooms to be taken literally so that we can claim that in heaven there is a literal physical house with many rooms so each disciple will have one? Or is this metaphorical language intended to communicate that each disciple will have a place in heaven? Does it even refer to a place apart from earth, or could it refer to having a place in the kingdom of God on earth?

John 14 tells the story of Jesus' last words to the disciples before his death. The resurrection has not yet occurred. He is offering comfort to his friends because he has declared that he must go away (John 13:33). John 14:2-3 offers not only the hope that they will one day be reunited, but that Jesus' departure will allow him to make that reunion possible.

Finally, the interpretation of Genesis 5:24 is at best a stretch. There is nothing in the text that suggests Enoch's body was transformed in anyway. Nor is there a clear statement that he went to heaven.[28] So, what do we conclude? Does the biblical text support the premillennial dispensational doctrine of rapture? It does only if select verses are pulled out of their literary context, braided together to create a new literary whole, and then read through the lens of premillennial dispensational presuppositions.

This doctrine of the rapture is played out vividly in volume 1 of the Left Behind fiction series, which is also entitled *Left Behind*. The story, however, left me wondering about the "tribulation saints," those who come to faith during the tribulation period that follows the rapture. What about these staunch believers who suffer torture, persecution, and even death for their commitment to Jesus?

Since the rapture ushers in a new situation, we might expect the people of faith in this new time to fall under a unique set of requirements. All that is said about this group is that they will be abundantly blessed.[29] It is what the story does not say about this group that is most interesting: it does not say that the tribulation saints share in being the bride of Christ (the marriage feast takes place right after the church is raptured); nor does it say that they will go to heaven. Apparently only those who are raptured by Jesus will participate in these wonderful events, suggesting that the doctrine of the rapture identifies and legitimates an elite group who will sit at the right hand of Jesus as his bride and receive glory and honor and power for eternity. This "first Second Coming" is said to be hidden, so members of the "true church" will know what happened, while the rest of the human population will be befuddled, not knowing how and why their loved ones have disappeared. The "second Second Coming," when Jesus comes to judge the wicked and set up his millennial kingdom after the tribulation, will be seen by all.[30] So the first second coming is for an elite group and that group, it appears, is made up of those who expect and prepare for the rapture, that is, the adherents of premillennial dispensationalism.

The Treaty Between the Antichrist and Israel

According to LaHaye and Jenkins, following the rapture of the true church, the Antichrist will initiate the tribulation period they believe is outlined in Revelation 6–16. He will do this by signing a "godless seven-year treaty" with the newly established Israel at the rebuilt temple. This event is played out in volume 2 of the Left Behind series, the *Tribulation Force*, and the notion is taken from the book of Daniel.[31]

Seventy weeks are decreed for your people and your holy city: to finish the transgression, to put an end to sin, and to atone for iniquity, to bring in everlasting righteousness, to seal both vision and prophet, and to anoint a most holy place. Know therefore and understand: from the time that the word went out to restore and rebuild Jerusalem until the time of an anointed prince, there shall be seven weeks; and for sixty-two weeks it shall be built again with streets and moat, but in a troubled time. After the sixty-two weeks, an anointed one shall be cut off and shall have nothing, and the troops of the prince who is to come shall destroy the city and the sanctuary. Its end shall come with a flood, and to the end there shall be war. Desolations are decreed. He shall make a strong covenant with many for one week, and for half of the week he shall make sacrifice and offering cease; and in their place shall be an abomination that desolates, until the decreed end is poured out upon the desolator. (Daniel 9:24-27)

LaHaye and Jenkins understand this passage to be entirely a pre-diction of Jesus and his second coming. To do this, they lump the seven weeks and the sixty-two weeks together to make one sixty-nine-week time period. Based on the assumption that "the time that the word went out to restore and rebuild Jerusalem" refers to Artaxerxes I sending Ezra to Jerusalem to reestablish the temple in 458 BCE (Ezra 7:1-6), they subtract 483 years (the sum of seven weeks of years plus sixty-two weeks of years) from that date to arrive at 25 CE.

LaHaye and Jenkins conclude that "*After* the appearance of Messiah as Ruler—483 years after the sixty-nine weeks have begun—he will be cut off."[32] By stating it this way, they insinuate that the beginning of the rule of the Messiah and the end (the time when he will be cut off) both come at the end of the 483 years. Thus they have interpreted these verses to refer to Jesus as the

THE FACTS BEHIND THE FICTION

Messiah (the Anointed One), who came to rule and was killed.

Finally, they state that 483 of the 490 years (the seventy "sevens") decreed for Daniel's people have elapsed and that a "divine counter" stopped just before the death of Jesus, leaving seven years remaining to fulfill the decree—a tribulation period that reflects the one-week (meaning seven years) "strong covenant" mentioned in Daniel 9:27. According to this interpretation, when the Antichrist signs the treaty with Israel, the divine counter will start ticking again and the final seven years will begin.[33]

In chapter 5, we took a careful look at Daniel and Revelation, the two books that play so central a role in the end-time scenario at the base of the Left Behind series. Let it suffice here, then, to begin with some background to this admittedly difficult text and then move to discussion of a few of the problems in the interpretation given by LaHaye and Jenkins. Essentially, the seventy weeks mentioned in Daniel 9:24 are an attempt by the writer to reinterpret Jeremiah's prediction that Judah will be exiled in Babylon for seventy years (Jeremiah 25:11-12; 29:10). In reality the exile lasted for about forty-nine years (from 587/6 to 538 BCE) when Persia conquered Babylon and King Cyrus decreed that the Jews were free to return to Jerusalem to rebuild the city and the temple (see, e.g., Ezra 1:1-3). The Daniel text extends the duration of the desolation in Jerusalem until the city and its temple were once again under Jewish control, which did not happen until 164 BCE when the Maccabees took back the temple and city by force. An annotated outline reflecting the historical situation follows.[34]

■ v. 25: From the time that the word went out to restore and rebuild Jerusalem (the decree of Cyrus in 538 BCE) until the time of an anointed prince (probable reference to the high priest Joshua or to Zerubbabel), there shall be seven weeks (equals 49 years; 7 x 7); and for sixty-two weeks (62 x 7 equals 434 years) Jerusalem shall be built again . . . but in a troubled time.

■ v. 26: After the sixty-two weeks, an anointed one shall be cut off (a reference to the murder of the high priest Onias III in 171 BCE), and the troops of the prince who is to come (Antiochus Epiphanes IV, ruler in the Seleucid Empire from 175–164 BCE) will destroy the city and the sanctuary.

■ v. 27: He will make a strong covenant with many (Antiochus Epiphanes IV entered into agreement with hellenizing Jews who lived in Jerusalem) for one week (seven years); and for half of the week (three and a half years) he shall make sacrifice and offering cease; and in their place shall be an abomination that desolates (Antiochus plundered the temple, disrupted the Jewish sacrificial system, and placed a statue of Zeus on the altar of sacrifice), until the decreed end is poured out upon the desolator (a prediction of the death of Antiochus Epiphanes IV).

The numbers of years do not add up exactly, but they seldom do in the Old Testament. It is best to think of biblical numbers and durations of time as rounded off and symbolic. For example, the Israelites were said to have wandered in the desert for forty years, which is a symbolic number in the Bible meaning "a long time." The "seventy weeks of years" in Daniel 9 has overtones of Leviticus 25–26, which describes a theology of Jubilee in which seven weeks of years (forty-nine years) was the maximum period of time that land could be kept from its ancestral heirs or that a person could be kept in slavery. In addition, in historical apocalypses, of which Daniel is one, the determinism of periods of history is a standard feature that often uses ten as a schematic number. Thus the symbolic 490 years in Daniel 9 is describing the duration of time for which Jerusalem was under the rule of another governmental power. Until the Maccabees took control of Jerusalem and the temple in 164 BCE, Jewish culture and worship were restricted. Once the Jewish people regained possession of Jerusalem and the temple, they experienced the Jubilee, the return of land to its rightful owner.

The interpretation given by LaHaye and Jenkins differs considerably from what I have outlined above. It also has some significant problems. The numbers in the LaHaye and Jenkins interpretation do not add up, so they invent the notion of a "divine counter" that stopped just before the death of Jesus, giving support to their preunderstanding of a seven-year period of tribulation. The statement that the counter stopped "just before the death of Jesus" is enigmatic. It is probably left unclear because Jesus did not die in 25 CE but a few years later. The only way to make sense of this interpretation is to read it through the lens of dispensationalism in general and Darbyite, futuristic, pretribulational, premillennial dispensationalism in particular. Why would the divine counter stop? The clock must stop ticking to fit in a seven-year tribulation, Where is such a concept found in Daniel? Nowhere. Where in the book of Revelation? Nowhere. It is contrived to build a bridge between Daniel 9 and the book of Revelation, but the bridge will not hold up when closely scrutinized.

Per their premillennial dispensational perspective, LaHaye and Jenkins call this interpretation of Daniel 9:23-27 a "literal" reading of the text, but there does not appear to be anything literal about it. Their interpretation requires significant changes or additions to the biblical text. While the text speaks of two messiahs, they speak of one. They combine the seven weeks and the sixty-two weeks of verse 25 into one unit so they can claim mention of only one messiah in the four verses. However, the Hebrew text clearly states two time periods of seven weeks and sixty-two weeks, respectively, which are separated by 434 years. After the first time period, the first messiah appears, and after the second time period, the second messiah appears. The two messiahs cannot refer to the same entity. The first period is when the word first went out to rebuild and restore Jerusalem, a reference to the decree of Cyrus in 538 BCE, which allowed the Jews to return to Jerusalem from their Babylonian exile. The second period is described in Daniel 9:26, where after the sixty-two weeks (434 years) an anointed one will be cut off. This reflects the historical period of persecution of the Jews by Antiochus Epiphanes IV (Daniel's context), which included the killing of Onias III and the desecration of the temple.

It is important to understand here the Hebrew text and issues related to translation. When the English says "anointed prince" or "anointed one" (Daniel 9:25–26), it is translating the Hebrew word *mashiah*. This Hebrew word is translated into Greek as *Christos*, the foundation for our English word *Christ*. In the Old Testament, the word *mashiah* appears thirty-eight times and refers most often to a historical human king, a few times to Samuel or a prophet, and once or twice to Israel. Each of these references is translated into English as "anointed" or "anointed one" and means someone anointed by God to lead and deliver the people from their enemies. It would be ludicrous, for example, to claim it refers to Jesus when King David is called *mashiah*. It is not until we get to the New Testament that "messiah" is limited to one person, Jesus of Nazareth. Consequently, "messiah" in Daniel 9:23-27 need not— in fact, ought not—be interpreted as a reference to Jesus.

The neglect of historical context for Daniel gives LaHaye and Jenkins free rein to name the *mashiah* and "anti-messiah" as they wish. Jesus is deemed the *mashiah* of Daniel, and the Antichrist mentioned in Revelation 6–16 is deemed to be the anti-messiah spoken of in Daniel 9:23-27. Hence Daniel 9:27 is forced into service to describe the initiation of a period of tribulation they say is spoken of in Revelation 6–16. This interpretation does violence to the text and ignores the use of the term *messiah* throughout the Old Testament.

Conclusions

It is clear that LaHaye and Jenkins support their understandings of what will happen before the period they call "the Tribulation" through questionable methodological practices. Let's revisit the doctrine of the rapture for a summary example of the problems inherent in this use of Scripture. None of the texts cited from Paul or the Gospel of John support the doctrine of the rapture. A close reading of the rapture text created by intermingling verses from 1 Thessalonians, 1 Corinthians, the Gospel of John, and Genesis has demonstrated that it does not support the doctrine of rapture unless it is read through the lens of the Israel-church dichotomy. In other words, the "literal" in "literal reading" of the texts depends on who is doing the evaluation. How, for instance, can any reader claim to know with certainty that being "made incorruptible by having our bodies made 'immortal'" (1 Corinthians 15:54) or "my Father's house of many rooms" (John 14:2-3) refers to a "true church" ascending to heaven, especially since the word *heaven* is not mentioned in either of the verses?

As noted in chapter 2, a characteristic of the premillennial dispensational system is the compartmentalization of Scripture with certain Scriptures determined to relate primarily to Israel while others relate primarily to the church. Given this practice of categorizing Scripture, LaHaye and Jenkins feel free to pull individual verses out of context and to weave them together to build doctrines. As Darbyite futurists, they pay little attention to the historical context from which biblical books come. Their selections as well as their interpretations are guided by a commitment to the presuppositions that the primary purpose of Scripture is to point toward the second coming of Jesus and that there is a distinction between Israel and the church. Their interpretations are defended by the claim of a literal reading of the Bible. These practices result in a one-dimensional reading of Scripture that disregards the unified history of God's interaction with the people that formed the Bible. In the next chapter, we will take a look at LaHaye and Jenkins's use and interpretation of the book of Revelation through the Left Behind series.

CHAPTER 7

The Left Behind Story and the Book of Revelation

No other single work has had as great an influence on the apocalyptic tradition as the book of Revelation. Its opening word, "apocalypse" or "revelation," which serves as a kind of self-designation, has become the name of a kind of writing and the ideas and themes associated with it. Although its key images have precedents in Jewish literature and parallels in other early Christian writings, it is from the book of Revelation that the popular images of "Armageddon," the "tribulation," the "millennium," and the "New Jerusalem" come.

—Adela Yarbro Collins, "The Book of Revelation,"
in *The Continuum History of Apocalypticism*

Everything we have discussed thus far has built to this moment. The goal of this chapter is to present and offer a critique of the essence of the original Left Behind series as it interprets the book of Revelation. This chapter begins with a summary of the story as it is told in the twelve volumes of the original series, then moves to an examination of several key events and characters and how the book of Revelation is appropriated by the authors to support the story line. The chapter closes with a discussion of the theological and methodological flaws in the treatment of Revelation by LaHaye and Jenkins to support those story elements.

125

THE FACTS BEHIND THE FICTION

yes!

Some readers may wonder why so much effort is being put into critiquing a *fiction* series. As mentioned in chapter 1, while Left Behind is indeed fiction, the novels reflect and promote a theological belief system that is held to be *the* truth by a small segment of the Christian community. Elements of their belief system have permeated Christian culture and the larger culture.

Left Behind tells the story of how the world as we know it will come to an end through divine intervention. The authors of the series believe such intervention is described in Revelation and other biblical texts. The story line of the series can be divided into three sections: events that lead up to the tribulation, the tribulation, and events that happen after the tribulation.

Chapter 6 presented a detailed look at the events that lead up to the tribulation. One of these events is purely fictional, and the rest draw only minimally on the book of Revelation: Revelation 3:10, "I will keep you from the hour of trial that is coming on the whole world," is used to support the idea of rapture; the command to measure the temple and altar of God (Revelation 11:1-2) is used to support the idea of a third temple; and the use of Babylon in Revelation 17–18 is used to support the idea of a rebuilt Babylon. The authors primarily support these notions with biblical texts found outside the book of Revelation or with an interpretation of combined biblical texts, as outlined in chapter 6.

Volume 12 of the series, *Glorious Appearing*, describes the end of the tribulation and the second coming of Jesus, followed by the sorting of the sheep and the goats in preparation for a millennial kingdom. These events are drawn from the authors' reading of Revelation. Volumes 2–11 of the series describe the tribulation itself and walk readers through Revelation 6–16. The following table[1] provides a summary of the events in the Left Behind story line as it unfolds in the novels. For a fuller treatment, readers may want to revisit the table found on page 5.

Book	Event	Scriptural Base
1 *Left Behind*	Rapture Seal judgment #1 Antichrist makes covenant with Israel The tribulation begins The two witnesses of Revelation begin their ministry	1 Thes 4:16-17; Rv 3:10 Rv 6:1-2 Dn 9:27 Rv 11:1-3
2 *Tribulation* *Force*	Seal judgment #2 Seal judgment #3	Rv 6:3-4 Rv 6:5-6
3 *Nicolae*	Seal judgment #4 Seal judgment #5 Seal judgment #6 Seal judgment #7	Rv 6:7-8 Rv 6:9-11 Rv 6:12-17; Rv 7:1-8 Rv 8:1-2
4 *Soul Harvest*	Trumpet judgment #1 Trumpet judgment #2 Trumpet judgment #3	Rv 8:7 Rv 8:8-9 Rv 8:10-11
5 *Apollyon*	Trumpet judgment #4 Trumpet judgment #5	Rv 8:12 Rv 9:1-11
6 *Assassins*	Trumpet judgment #6 Trumpet judgment #7	Rv 9:13-19 Rv 11:15-19
7 *The Indwelling*	The mark of the Beast begins	Rv 13:16-18
8 *The Mark*	Midpoint of the tribulation	
9 *Desecration*	Antichrist desecrates the temple Bowl judgment #1 Bowl judgment #2	Dn 9:27; Mt 24:15 Rv 16:2 Rv 16:3
10 *The Remnant*	Bowl judgment #3 Bowl judgment #4	Rv 16:4-7 Rv 16:8-9
11 *Armageddon*	Bowl judgment #5 Bowl judgment #6 Battle of Armageddon	Rv 16:10-11 Rv 16:12 Rv 19:19-21
12 *Glorious* *Appearing*	Return of Christ to earth Bowl judgment #7 Beast and False Prophet thrown in to the lake of fire Satan bound in the Abyss The millennial kingdom— Christ rules from Jerusalem But after these things [Satan] must be released for a little while	Rv 19:11-21 Rv 16:17-21 Rv 19:20 Rv 20:1-3 Rv 20:4-6 Rv 20:3

Events and Characters

The best way to understand the narrative of the Left Behind series is to begin with a look at the key characters and events through which the story unfolds.

The 144,000: People of Jewish descent who come to faith in Jesus as the Christ and become the great evangelists of the tribulation.

Bruce Barnes: A visitation pastor who does not get taken in the rapture, although his family does. Bruce comes to faith in Christ after viewing a videotape left by the senior pastor that explains all the end-time events. He then brings to Christ Rayford Steele, Buck Williams, and Chloe Steele, who form the Tribulation Force under his leadership.

Tsion Ben-Judah: A well-known and accomplished rabbinical scholar who is hired by the Hebrew Institute of Biblical Research to study messianic Scriptures. After announcing his conclusions on international television, he becomes the spiritual leader and teacher of the Tribulation Force.

Great soul harvest: Before the world experiences the sixth seal judgment at the end of the first quarter of the tribulation, God will raise up an army of 144,000 Jewish evangelists who will win more men and women to Christ than have been won during any other time in history.

Old Testament saints: Those who died before Jesus came to earth but were justified by faith, for example, Enoch, Noah, and Abraham (Hebrews 11:4-12).

Operation Eagle: A rescue mission in which one million Jews are airlifted to Petra, an ancient Jordanian city, which serves as the new home for the Jewish remnant during the tribulation until Jesus appears. In the later volumes, Petra also eventually becomes the center for Chaim Rosenzweig's and Tsion Ben-Judah's ministries, as well as the militaristic outpost of the Tribulation Force.

Chaim Rosenzweig: A Nobel Prize–winning Israeli botanist and statesman who becomes a Christian after killing Nicolae Carpathia (the Antichrist); later on in the series, he negotiates the departure of messianic Jews from Israel, leading them to safety in Petra.

Rayford Steele: Former 747 pilot for Pan-Continental and one of four original members of the Tribulation Force. He becomes the force's leader after the death of Bruce Barnes. He functions in a dual role as the pilot for Global Community potentate Nicolae Carpathia and as the leader of the Tribulation Force throughout much of the series.

Tribulation Force: People of both Jewish and Gentile descent who ban together to create safe houses for believers and organize the fight against the Antichrist.

Tribulation martyrs: People of both Jewish and Gentile descent who are murdered because of their Christian witness.

Tribulation saints: People of both Jewish and Gentile descent who come to faith in Jesus as the Christ after the rapture has taken place and who die during the tribulation.

Two witnesses: Two men dressed in sackcloth who stand at the Wailing Wall in Jerusalem for 1,260 days performing impossible feats and sharing prophecies that are understood by everyone in their own languages; these two are either a reincarnation of Moses and Elijah or the Old Testament characters themselves.

The key negative characters and events in the Left Behind story are:

Nicolae Jetty Carpathia: Former president of Romania and former secretary-general of the United Nations who becomes the self-appointed potentate of the Global Community (GC). He is assassinated in Jerusalem and resurrected at the GC Palace in New Babylon. He is the Antichrist, the embodiment of the first beast described in Revelation 13:1-10.

Leon Fortunato: The Antichrist Carpathia's right-hand man, who bears the title Supreme Commander. He is the embodiment of the second beast, the False Prophet, described in Revelation 13:11-18, and he orders the world to worship the Antichrist.

The Global Community: The name of the one-world empire that is led by the Antichrist, Nicolae Jetty Carpathia, with its headquarters in New Babylon.

New Babylon: Described as the most magnificent city ever built, it is built over the ruins of historic Babylon and is located in current-day Iraq, about fifty-six miles south of Baghdad. As the capital of the world—the center of banking, commerce, and government—it is the new holy city and becomes the headquarters of the Global Community and the Antichrist.

The Tribulation Story Line

Shortly after the rapture takes place, four Gentiles come to faith in Jesus. These four form the Tribulation Force, a team whose task is to fight the enemies of God and provide protection and resources for the believing community during the seven chaotic years of the tribulation. As the series moves along, the force gathers more and more members. When things begin to heat up in the tribulation, the Tribulation Force decides to go underground. Initially they move to safe houses—first to the home of one of the Tribulation Force members, then to Chicago, and finally to San Diego. When the San Diego safe house is compromised, the Tribulation Force moves to the ancient city of Petra, where they establish a technology-driven militaristic outpost. The establishment of the compound at Petra represents the authors' recasting of the flight to the desert of the woman clothed with the sun as found in Revelation 12. At Petra the 144,000 Jewish witnesses are protected along with their new Jewish converts, and the Gentile members of the Tribulation Force take arms, preparing themselves for battle with the Antichrist and his armies.

Meanwhile, the Antichrist, Nicolae Jetty Carpathia, is establishing what comes to be known as the Global Community, with headquarters in recently built New Babylon. The Global Community becomes a world empire, supporting a one-world government, economy, and religion. Although not clearly stated as such, the story line seems to associate Carpathia, New Babylon, and the establishment of the Global Community as depictions of the Antichrist from Revelation 13, and Rome and the Roman Empire as depicted in Revelation 17–18. Carpathia's faithful sidekick, Leon Fortunato, who began as supreme commander, eventually becomes the Most High Reverend Father of Carpathianism. As such, Fortunato proclaims Carpathia as the risen God who is to be worshiped. To achieve this end, Fortunato has an image of Carpathia erected in Jerusalem and forces everyone, under threat of death, to bow down to it. Fortunato seems to be associated with the second beast, the beast of the land found in Revelation 13:11-18, who is also called the False Prophet, a title the Tribulation Force adopts as a nickname for Fortunato about midway through the series.

In Jerusalem the third temple has been completed, which thrills the Jewish people. There are several significant Jewish characters in the story. Dr. Chaim Rosenzweig, is a Nobel Prize–winning Israeli botanist who invents a formula that Israel uses to make the desert bloom and the country flourish, which becomes the impetus for an attack by Russia as discussed in chapter 6. Dr. Rosenzweig eventually assassinates Carpathia, who in turn rises from the dead on the third day—which is likely intended to mimic the healing of the Beast found in Revelation 13:3.

The second significant Jewish character is Tsion Ben-Judah, a rabbinical scholar and Israeli statesman hired by the Hebrew Institute of Biblical Research to study the requirements for the Messiah as recorded in the Scriptures. After a year of studying prophecy, and in an attempt to interpret the events of his day, he concludes that Jesus is the Messiah after all and reveals this conclusion on national television. As a result, many Jews come to faith in Jesus as Messiah, and Ben-Judah becomes the spiritual leader and teacher for the Tribulation Force. His teachings are broadcast through cyberspace, and he gains a daily audience of more than one billion readers. Toward the end of the series, Ben-Judah teaches the Jewish community housed at Petra and ultimately meets his death defending the Old City in Jerusalem. Rosenzweig and Ben-Judah have no counterparts in the book of Revelation. Their characters have been created to fill in gaps in a story line that is based on more than the book of Revelation.

Contributing to the numbers of people who come to faith in Jesus throughout the tribulation—the great soul harvest—are the two witnesses who stand at the Wailing Wall. They speak in pithy statements that proclaim the truth, foretell the future, warn the elect, and evangelize unbelievers. The two witnesses are presented in the series literally as Moses and Elijah, who were known for their campaigns against idolatry. They are protected by God until they are murdered, and their bodies are left in the street for all to see. After three and a half days they are resurrected, and they eventually ascend into heaven. LaHaye and Jenkins say the witnesses are allowed to be killed for reasons "known only to God."[2] These characters closely follow Revelation chapter 11:1-14, except in their identification as Moses and Elijah.

During the fifth trumpet judgment, which is drawn from Revelation 9:1-11, Ben-Judah addresses the 144,000, who are Jewish evangelists who will bring in the great soul harvest. The 144,000, along with all the Jesus-followers, receive a seal on their foreheads. This seal looks like a relief of a cross but is visible only to fellow believers. The seal appears from nowhere and is noticed one day by those in the Tribulation Force. The seals serve to protect the 144,000, and all believers, from spiritual harm, although physically they can still be injured. The believers' seal is a physical literal interpretation of Revelation 7:1-8.

Many of the believers die in the course of the Left Behind story. In fact, by the end of the series, only one of the original four Tribulation Force members is left standing. When asked about this,

Jerry Jenkins said that according to figures extrapolated from the book of Revelation, one-fourth of the population remaining after the rapture will survive the tribulation.[3]

Carpathia's resurrection from the dead is paralleled with the Revelation 12:7-9 battle in the heavens between Michael the archangel and Satan and his angels. Satan loses the war and is thrown to the earth, and according to the story, indwells the Antichrist, who comes back to life at that moment. After Carpathia is resurrected from the dead, he requires all faithful citizens of the Global Community to receive a mark as a sign of loyalty to him and to his world empire. In contrast to the seal of God, this mark is physically administered by Carpathia's workers and is visible to everyone. A special guillotine is set in the public square to behead those who refuse the mark, so they can serve as an example. Carpathia's mark represents the mark of the Beast found in Revelation 13:16-17.

Carpathia's resurrection and indwelling take place at the midpoint of the seven years of tribulation and signal the beginning of the second half of the tribulation, which is called the "Great Tribulation." The Great Tribulation is initiated by the desecration of the temple by the Antichrist. More will be said about the Great Tribulation in the critique section of this chapter.

The Glorious Appearing

The original twelve-volume Left Behind series concludes with the second coming of Jesus. According to LaHaye and Jenkins, there are 318 New Testament predictions of Jesus' return, making this belief the cornerstone of the Christian faith.[4] Based on Zechariah 14:3-5, they believe that when Jesus returns he will return to the Mount of Olives from which he left. Drawing from a variety of texts, they identify four campaigns that Jesus will then engage. First he will go to Edom to rescue Israel (Isaiah 63:1-6). Second, he will defeat the armies of the world at the Valley of Megiddo (Revelation

16:12-16). Third, he will defeat the remainder of the world's evil forces at the Valley of Jehoshaphat (Joel 3:1-2, 9-17; Revelation 14:14-20). Finally, he will come to Jerusalem to defeat the advance guard of the Antichrist, who will attempt to wipe out the Holy City (Zechariah 12:1-9; Revelation 16:17-21).[5] These battles play out in interesting ways in *Armageddon* and *Glorious Appearing*.

The glorious appearing, or return of Jesus, begins with an illuminated cross appearing in the clouds as Carpathia and his armies are marching toward Petra. When the armies arrive, they are unable to do anything—their bullets and swords have no effect as the Tribulation Force walks right through their attacks unharmed. And then darkness fills the sky. The darkness is interrupted by the opening of the heavens and the appearance of Jesus on a white horse, which is a depiction of Revelation 19:11-21. When Jesus speaks, tens of thousands of Carpathia's men fall dead. Soon after, the Jewish remnant at Petra begins their journey to Jerusalem, where Jesus will gather them together, and where Carpathia's troops will continue to attack them, but with no success.

Based on Daniel 12:11-12, the story line sees a 75-day gap between the glorious appearing and the beginning of the millennial reign. Daniel 12:11 indicates that there will be 1,290 days between the abomination of desolation and the end of the great persecution, while Daniel 12:12 says, "Happy are those who persevere and attain the thousand three hundred thirty-five days." They take these verses as a reference to a future millennial kingdom and the time that immediately precedes it. Subtracting the 1,260 days their story gives between the desolation and the glorious appearing (lifted from Revelation 11:3 and 12:6) from the number in Daniel 12:11 (1,290), they are left with 30 days. To these 30 days, they add 45, which represents the difference between the two sets of days numbered in Daniel 12:11-12, and thus arrive at a period of 75 days, during which Jesus will be preparing the temple as described in Ezekiel 40–48.[6]

When it comes to the millennium, the novel leaves no stone unturned. It addresses who will be married in the millennium, whether children will be born, and if so, whether they will be believers. However, it is in the presentation of the resurrections and judgments that we get a clear picture of the authors' premillennial dispensational beliefs. Revelation refers to two resurrections: a resurrection to life (20:5-6) and a resurrection of judgment, or "the second death," found in Revelation 20:11-15. According to the Left Behind series, all the redeemed throughout the ages will participate in the resurrection to life, but the timing of each person's resurrection varies. There are three categories: Old Testament saints, those who have been raptured (both those who were resurrected from the dead at the time of the rapture and those who were alive at the time of the rapture—LaHaye and Jenkins's commitment to a "literal" reading means they must include both groups under this category, although theoretically those who were alive at the time of the rapture are never resurrected), and Christians martyred during the tribulation (includes tribulation saints). (People of faith who live through the tribulation and are alive at the time of the millennium will be resurrected at the end of the millennium.) According to the authors, Christians who die before the rapture, the "dead in Christ," will be resurrected at the rapture, but the Old Testament saints will not. The Old Testament saints will not be resurrected until the period of judgment that accompanies Jesus' return and preparation for the millennial kingdom. (This stands in contrast to Scofield's conclusion, that all the saved are included in the first resurrection.)

Several judgments are also presented in *Glorious Appearing*. Those who remain alive after the tribulation, about a fourth of those left after the rapture, are gathered at the Valley of Jehoshaphat so Jesus can prepare for the millennial reign. When they arrive, they are sorted into three groups: the goats (the followers of the Antichrist), the sheep (Gentile followers of Jesus who have honored the Jews), and the brethren (Jewish followers of Jesus). After quoting many

Scripture texts, Jesus waves his hands and the ground opens up to consume the goats, who are sent to Hades to await the resurrection unto judgment at the close of the millennium, at which time they will participate in the great white throne judgment.

Believers are judged according to their sins and works in four different groupings, depending on whether they are Old Testament saints, tribulation saints (including tribulation martyrs), Jews still alive at the end of the tribulation, or Gentiles still alive at the end of the tribulation. After dealing with the goats at the Valley of Jehoshaphat, all who have died in faith but were not taken in the rapture come from the earth and the heavens to gather around the throne of Jesus. Each group is then brought before the throne to be honored: first the Old Testament saints, then the tribulation martyrs, and finally the tribulation saints. The tribulation itself is the time of judgment for the Jews still alive at the end of the tribulation, the time for Israel to "pass under the rod" (Ezekiel 20:37 KJV). Two-thirds of Israel dies before the millennium, and based on the authors' understanding of Zechariah 13, all who remain will be saved and enter into a new covenant with God. In the novel, Chaim, one of the Jewish leaders, credits the Gentiles with the conversion of the Jews.[7] The Gentiles still alive at the end of the tribulation will be judged at the judgment seat of Christ, understood to be a unique judgment for believers. This will happen just before the millennium begins.

The raptured group, the true church, however, is missing from this time of judgment because they have already stood before the judgment seat of Christ, after which they were adorned as the bride of Christ and prepared to descend with him at the glorious appearing. In the final pages of the novel, those who were raptured appear in their glorified bodies to have fellowship with their loved ones. All believers from every age are present at this reunion, where they engage one another in conversation and even hug. This is how the book ends.

Critique ✓

While the appropriation and presentation of the book of Revelation in the Left Behind story line raise numerous issues, the following critique focuses on issues of primary interest: the rapture and a two-part, seven-year tribulation with an indwelt Antichrist; the global community; the military outpost at Petra; the desecration of the temple; and the Israel-church divide. The interpretation of Revelation that forms the basis for Left Behind is driven by three assumptions: that 28 percent of the Bible is prophetic prediction of the initial and second comings of Jesus; that human history is divided into dispensations in which God deals with people in different ways; and that biblical text is to be read literally whenever possible. These three theological and methodological commitments allow LaHaye, Jenkins, and other premillennial dispensationalists to ignore the time, culture, context, and artistry of the biblical text and to import texts from one biblical book into another to create new meaning, as if all the biblical texts are speaking about the same thing. LaHaye and Jenkins have done this with Revelation by importing notions developed from Daniel 9, Matthew 24, and 1 Thessalonians 4 to create a story line that no longer emphasizes nonviolent resistance, but instead emphasizes militaristic resistance. This is a lot of change for one little biblical book, and the implications are far-reaching.

The Rapture and Seven-Year Tribulation

As explained in chapter 6, the authors claim that 1 Thessalonians 4:16-17 and Revelation 3:10 provide evidence for "the Rapture." Revelation 3:10 is in fact the only reference made in the Left Behind novels to the letters to the seven churches, although the ills addressed in these seven letters are evident throughout the novels. Readers will recall that the common concern addressed in the letters to the seven churches is the practice of idolatry. Revelation 3:10 is a part of the letter to the Philadelphia church, and it affirms the community members for their faithfulness in the midst of persecution, in spite of their limited powers. Consequently, the community is assured that they will be kept from "the hour of trial that is coming on the whole world." LaHaye and Jenkins read this to mean removal prior to the time of trial. The context of the entire letter, however, indicates that the Christians in this community will not be removed from the times of trial, but rather will be sustained through them. This is evident in verse 12, which has the following conditional clause: "If you conquer, I will make you a pillar in the temple of my God."

LaHaye and Jenkins also impose on the book of Revelation ideas developed from Daniel 9:24-27 of a seven-year tribulation that is kicked off by a covenant between the Antichrist and Israel. These ideas are an affront to the message of Revelation because they give no credence to the historical context from which the book flows. Written after the Jewish revolt of 66–70 CE, which ended with the destruction of the second temple, Revelation does not predict a time when tribulation will begin. Rather, it responds to the tribulations of the time, namely, the intense sustained persecution that culminated in the destruction of the temple (due to the revolt) and the sporadic persecution that continued until John's day, some of which John himself had experienced and which he anticipated would become even more severe.

According to LaHaye and Jenkins, the seven-year tribulation is broken into two halves, with the second three-and-a-half-year period being the "Great Tribulation." This seven-year period is developed from Daniel 9:24-27, as outlined in chapter 6. Readers will recall that the authors believe the Antichrist will make a covenant with Israel, after which the "divine clock" will start ticking once again to count down the final seven years of history. Revelation has three sets of seven judgments, the flow of which is interrupted by two different interludes (Revelation 7:1-8 and 10:1–11:13). After the second interlude, which states that the current judgment is not final, LaHaye and Jenkins discern a midpoint in the tribulation, during which, they claim, the Antichrist is indwelt by Satan, and thus the "Great Tribulation" begins.

The concept of the indwelling of the Antichrist is problematic for several reasons. Nowhere does the Bible suggest that Satan will indwell the Antichrist. Further, this concept of the indwelling constitutes a chronology in which the future midtribulational indwelling is paralleled with Satan being defeated and thrown to earth after Jesus has been taken to heaven (Revelation 12). However, one of the major points of Revelation is that the battle between God and Satan was won by the blood of the Lamb, and so the defeat of Satan, according to Revelation, happened immediately following Jesus' historic ascension into heaven—it is not a future event!

Additionally, although John's symbolic use of Daniel's three-and-a-half-year schema (Revelation 11:3 and 12:6) to suggest a period of intense persecution for his own generation is symbolic, Daniel's three and a half years reflected actual events and hope for deliverance during a time of persecution under Antiochus Epiphanes IV. John of Patmos is borrowing language from the book of Daniel to talk about the evils of his own time, namely, the economic, military, and political oppression of Rome.

LaHaye and Jenkins's interpretation of Daniel 9:24-27 ignores the passage's historical context as much as their imposition of the Daniel passage on Revelation ignores the historical context of 66–100 CE. By doing so, LaHaye and Jenkins are able to say that both books speak primarily of things to come. While it is clear the prediction of the end of the persecutions for Daniel and John had not yet been realized at the time of their writing, significant portions of Daniel and Revelation describe events from the historical time period from which they come. To ignore the references in these books to the actual historical circumstances of the writers and first readers/hearers is to claim that their main messages were intended only for you and me today. This neglects the truth that the writings were prepared for a particular people, our spiritual ancestors, who underwent significant persecution for their faith for which they needed a word of hope and direction. These are the witnesses who, by the grace of God, remained faithful to the point of death. As inheritors of the faith these witnesses helped to sustain, we owe them the honor of respecting their crises and their efforts to remain faithful and the acknowledgment that Daniel and Revelation first belonged to them. While these two biblical books have much to say to us today, we must ever bear in mind that we are but one generation among many served by their inspiration, hope, and guidance.

The Global Community

LaHaye and Jenkins understand that Daniel's vision of the statue made of different metals (2:31-45) is symbolic of four successive world empires (Babylon, Media/Persia, Hellenistic (Greek) Empire, Rome). The four beasts of Daniel 7 represent the same four world empires, yet when John of Patmos uses the imagery of the four beasts to create his composite character of the beast that rises from the sea (Revelation 13), LaHaye and Jenkins don't connect the dots. Instead, they take the reference to Babylon as literal. As outlined in chapter 5, John's beast from the sea represents Rome, and the Antichrist most likely represents the emperor Nero.

Simultaneously, the authors turn to Daniel 9:26-27 and read the phrase "the troops of the prince who is to come shall destroy the city and the sanctuary" as referring to the destruction of the second temple by the Romans in 70 CE. From this they conclude that the Antichrist will be from Romania, "a former eastern-bloc country that retains much of its Roman heritage."[8] As is also noted in chapter 5, this phrase from Daniel 9:26-27 refers to the armies of Antiochus Epiphanes IV (167-164 BCE). While LaHaye and Jenkins seemingly cannot comprehend the historical realities to which Daniel's and John's images point, they *are* able to make interpretive associations of these images to contemporary and/or future events. They understand that Revelation is critiquing the religious, social, political, and economic activities of a world power, and so they created a similar story line in the Left Behind series; and in so doing, they have ended up predicting that the past will be re-created in the future so every prophecy written in the Bible can be fulfilled.

Finally, the destruction of Rome and the return of Jesus coincide in Revelation (chaps. 17–20). This creates a problem for the literal interpretive practice of LaHaye and Jenkins—we live in a time when Rome has been destroyed but Jesus has not yet returned. Although the authors do not interpret Babylon as Rome in the book of Revelation, they understand the fourth beast of Daniel to be Rome and believe that Jesus will come simultaneous to Rome's destruction.[9] The authors solve the dilemma their befuddled interpretations have created by suggesting that we are still living in the time of the Roman Empire: "Today, even though Rome is no longer an empire, virtually all western nations have taken their basic principles of government from Rome. The Laws, statutes, senate, and other debating bodies have continued in what is called 'Cesarean imperialism.'"[10] So, in their thinking, contemporary people are the ones who will see the coming of the Antichrist, as he takes over the world, establishes a one-world economy, proclaims himself God, desecrates a rebuilt temple, and rules from a rebuilt Babylon. Those of us in this generation who are true believers can expect to be snatched away while the rest suffer the tribulation and await the Jesus who will come on a white horse to judge and to save. And according to the authors, we will see this soon. They envision a move to a one-world economy in the European Common Market. They claim Babylon is already being rebuilt. And they tell of the Jewish community planning for a third temple and the reimplementation of sacrifices. They name the contemporary liberalization and secularization of the church as the foundation to the coming one-world religion. "Yes," they say, "no generation of Christians ever had more reason for believing [Jesus] could come in their lifetime than does ours!"[11]

The Military Outpost at Petra
LaHaye and Jenkins take a huge leap into symbolic interpretation in their explanation of the outpost at Petra. This story element is drawn from their interpretation of Revelation 12:13-14, which describes the woman clothed with the sun fleeing the dragon by receiving wings and flying into the wilderness where she would be safe and nourished for three and a half years. LaHaye and Jenkins recast this scene of the woman flying to safety in a twenty-first-century, high-tech militaristic operation. While the image of the people of faith fleeing to the desert for safety is an acceptable interpretation of the imagery of the woman clothed with the sun, the establishment of a high-tech military compound is not. The book of Revelation does not contain within it a call to arms, and it does not contain any examples of human combat. The imposition of military preparations and strategies on the image of the woman fleeing to the desert does serious violence to the biblical text and can easily lead readers of the fiction series, which is touted as presenting biblical truth, to believe that Daniel and Revelation are a call to arms.

The Temple
The impetus for book 9 of the Left Behind series, in which the Antichrist enters and desecrates the temple, comes from Daniel 9:27 and Matthew 24:15. LaHaye and Jenkins predict that the Antichrist will enter the newly built third temple at the midpoint of the tribulation and desecrate it by offering a pig on the altar. He will persecute the faithful Jews by demanding veneration of a statue of himself. But desecrations and persecutions have already happened and on more than one occasion—first, by Antiochus Epiphanes IV (167–164 BCE), then during the destruction of the second temple in 70 CE. Daniel 9:27 and Matthew 24:15 describe these violations.

In contrast, the book of Revelation says nothing about the desecration or destruction of the temple. The closest reference is in 11:11-12, where John is told not to measure the court outside the temple because it has been given over to the nations who will trample the holy city but no mention is made of desecration. In fact, the point seems to be that John has outlined a way to protect the temple, a means of spiritual protection for the faithful during persecution. The image of the temple is just that, an image, evidenced by Revelation 21:22, which clearly states, "I saw no temple in the city, for its temple is the Lord God the Almighty and the Lamb." One of the most significant messages of the book is that a temple is not needed because the glory of God permeates the entire community.

The Israel-Church Divide
That LaHaye and Jenkins are wholeheartedly committed to the premillennial dispensational doctrine of the Israel and church divide is very apparent in the judgments outlined in the final volume of the series. Close scrutiny of the story line reveals the belief that an elite group of Christians will be raptured and become the bride of Christ. The Old Testament saints and martyrs and the tribulation saints and martyrs will reign with Jesus in the millennial kingdom, while the bride of Christ will return by his side at the glorious appearing. The Jewish and Gentile survivors of the tribulation will be the subjects of the kingdom, in which the believing Jews will hold a higher status. This theology is not present in the book of Revelation or elsewhere in the Bible. In fact, John of Patmos went to great lengths through his use of twelve twelves, which represent the tribes of Israel and the apostles, to emphasize a unified faith community. Similarly while most biblical interpreters understand "there was a great multitude that no one could count, from every nation" (Revelation 7:9) to be an explanation of the gathering of the 144,000, LaHaye and Jenkins say this verse is describing a second group, and they maintain that the 144,000 (Revelation 7:4-14) are all Jewish.

Summary

The implications of the interpretive methods LaHaye and Jenkins have applied to Revelation are significant. First, by weaving numerous biblical texts together and creating a fictional story line to communicate their interpretation, they have shifted the fundamental message of John of Patmos away from nonviolent resistance to a call to arms. The Left Behind series does not teach the power of suffering love as revealed through the cross but instead promotes a message of military resistance.

Second, by creating a story that rests on the imposed notion of the rapture, the authors ignore the clear message of Revelation's twelve twelves and foment a division between Jews and Gentiles. They create a class of elite Christians who can expect special treatment and function within a second-level leadership rung, ruling with Jesus over a two-tiered citizenry of Jews and Gentiles who can, at best, hope for a secondary reward. The book of Revelation does not support such a "them and us" mind-set.

Finally, the insistence on what LaHaye and Jenkins call a "literal" interpretation of the book of Revelation creates far more confusion than clarity as well as an inconsistent new mythology rather than a respectful acceptance of Scripture on its own terms. While the reference to Babylon in Revelation translates into a new Babylon, the woman dressed with the sun translates into a modern-day high-tech militaristic outpost in an ancient city. Babylon will be re-created while Petra was created for the purpose of housing a Jewish remnant in some future time. This theology creates and sustains an overly mythological perspective that presents everything with a secret purpose that relates to some future Jesus moment. The past and present are lost to the future. What ever happened to today?

CHAPTER 8

Implications for the Church

An eschatology which is expressed in terms of historic development has no final consummation. Its consummations are always the basis for further development. The Kingdom of God is always coming. . . . If [God] called humanity to a halt in a "kingdom of glory," he would have on his hands some millions of eager spirits whom he has himself trained to ceaseless aspiration and achievement, and they would be dying of ennui. . . . [But] we are on the march toward the Kingdom of God, and getting our reward by every fractional realization of it which makes us hungry for more. A stationary humanity would be a dead humanity. The life of the race is in its growth.

—Walter Rauschenbusch,
A Theology for the Social Gospel

The Theology

John of Patmos believed the events leading up to and surrounding the fall of Jerusalem and the subsequent persecution of the Christians were signs of the immediate end of the world as he knew it. The author of Daniel believed the same thing about 250 years earlier as he witnessed the persecutions of the Jews and the desecration of Jerusalem and the temple mount by Antiochus Epiphanes IV. This is a common theme in biblical literature. Paul and the Gospel writers share John's and Daniel's anticipation for the end of their current distress as they look for the return of Jesus (*parousia*) in their own lifetimes.

It should be clear by now that the Christian church has never been in total agreement about what will happen in the course of history. Some, such as the premillennial dispensationalists, map out in great detail events of the end of human history. Others find the books of Daniel and Revelation to contain much symbolism and conclude that their depictions of the end are written in symbolic language. Historically, Christianity has not taught that the kingdom was delayed, rather that it has been fulfilled in the church. The kingdom of heaven has come; it is here and now. We are experiencing the kingdom of heaven through the life of the church. At the same time, the church has consistently looked to the future for something more; the faithful have hoped for a new and just social order. Although the faithful may die a physical death, the hope has been that God would gather the community of faith from every era together to celebrate and sustain this new social order.

Fundamentally, biblical apocalyptic literature (Daniel, Revelation, and sections of Isaiah, Ezekiel, Zechariah, Matthew, Mark, and First and Second Thessalonians) is resistance literature, which presumes the existence of a faithful remnant who will endure the oppressions and persecutions of their time. Evil is overcome through the power of nonviolent resistance. Through faithful obedience to the Law, as in the book of Daniel, or to Christ, as in Revelation, evil will be defeated. The key to this theology is nonparticipation in evil. In the case of Revelation, Jesus, the slain Lamb, is the true victor, and the battle between good and evil is essentially over. It only remains for the Christ-followers to gain victory on earth through their faithful endurance and witness.

The Call

Other apocalypses were written during the second temple period that are not in the Bible, but they are responses to the same crises that Daniel and Revelation address. Not unlike responses to crises in our contemporary world, these writings vary significantly in perspective.[1] The diversity of responses includes the call to militaristic campaigns; a condemnation of Gentile/Greek and Roman religious, political, and cultural practices; the questioning of God's justice; a pondering of the human propensity for sin; and unequivocal statements of God's future retributive justice. Only one response, however, remains in both the Catholic and Protestant canons. That is nonviolent resistance, as found in the books of Daniel and Revelation. Daniel and Revelation do not question the justice of God. They acknowledge but do not emphasize the sin(s) of the people. And they do not call the faith community to arms. These two apocalypses, which are held to be authoritative, assume the existence of a faithful remnant who will bear witness while enduring persecution and oppression and remain faithful even unto death.

A critical distinction, then, between the premillennial dispensational view of the Left Behind series and the view presented in this book, is how the community of faith is called to resist evil. In Left Behind, there is the escape of true believers through the rapture, which is followed by armed resistance as symbolized in the Tribulation Force, rather than the commission to endure and overcome through nonparticipation in evil and active witness to Jesus. One question that begs to be addressed is what exactly the remnant is being called to resist—how do we define *evil*? It should come as no surprise that not everyone gives the same answer.

Resisting Evil

For premillennial dispensational "prophecy teachers" who believe there are more than one hundred Old Testament prophecies that have been fulfilled by the life of Jesus Christ, three hundred predictions that they believe have not yet been fulfilled are of great interest. Some believe many of the unfulfilled predictions are beginning to come to pass today; others are looking for signs that they will come to pass in the near future. They are all looking for developments in the Middle East and Europe, the rebuilding of cities and structures, and the development of governmental, economic, and religious structures to match those spoken of in the Bible. For example, a report titled "Europe Unites as a Powerful Empire" proclaims that the second chapter of Daniel predicted a reunited Roman Empire in the "End Times" and the uniting of Europe is evidence of that prediction coming to pass.[2] However, as outlined in chapter 5, many of the events the premillennial dispensational prophecy teachers are looking for have already taken place, so it is wasted energy to look for them to occur in our times or in the future. Looking to events around the globe as supernatural signs of the coming kingdom also means overlooking the role—and responsibility—the church has for ushering in that kingdom and thus changes the mission of the church.

One aspect of apocalyptic literature that is often seen as a sign of "the end" is natural disasters. There will always be natural disasters, and to try to interpret them in light of apocalyptic literature would be unreasonable. The descriptions of earthquakes in the Bible, for example, are used in various ways and ought not to be understood as evidence in our contemporary world that the end is near or as God's judgment on the victims. In Amos 1:1 an earthquake is used as a historical marker. In several Old and New Testament passages (Psalm 29:6, 8; 104:32; Isaiah 29:6; Matthew 27:54; 28:2; Acts 16:26), earthquakes are a positive sign of God's presence. The gospel writers speak of earthquakes as the beginning of the "birthpangs"—preliminary stages to the end—not evidence of the end itself (Matthew 24:8; Mark 13:8; Luke 21:9–11). In Revelation we find one of the rare instances, if not the only instance, where earthquakes are specifically described as judgments.

Other "signs of the end" that premillennial dispensationalists tout are the move toward a one-world government, religion, and economy through the United Nations, the European World Market, and the creation of international trade agreements; the development of technology with the potential to run a one-world empire; the cries for world peace and religious tolerance; the threat of World War III; the rise of socialism and communism; and an increase of plagues and viruses. LaHaye and Jenkins have created a great deal of hype around these signs and have brought their scenario to life through the story line of the Left Behind series, while reassuring the "believing" community of supernatural removal from harm's way. Anyone who believes outside the structure of premillennial dispensationalism is at best suspect and at worst evil. This perspective keeps believers fearful that they might slip into the wrong camp, which does tremendous damage to individual believers, to the universal Christian church, to our nation, and to the world by creating a fear and disdain for the "other." The sense of crisis inherent in this view leads some to an inward, self-protective focus, as threatening circumstances always do, and ultimately the New Testament commitments to love of neighbor and love of enemies are lost. In other words, the gospel message is truncated. In the end, the hungry are not fed, the thirsty are not given water, the stranger is not welcomed, the naked are not clothed, the sick are not cared for, and prisoners are not visited (Matthew 25:35-46). Instead, they are only proselytized. It is the gospel mandate to care for the poor, receive the stranger, and love both neighbor and enemy that is left behind.

For Christians, being faithful witnesses means living out and proclaiming the core message of the gospel of Jesus Christ, which for the pure premillennial dispensationalist is "Proclaim and prepare for the second coming of Jesus!" Resisting evil for them means separating from the world, ostracizing those who think differently, and adhering to rigid rules of personal conduct. In contrast, the broader Christian community believes in at least some degree of tolerance for diversity among believers. Living the gospel includes feeding the hungry, clothing the naked, caring for the sick, and visiting prisoners. So remaining faithful to the end includes resisting the evil social structures that oppress the poor and needy and working, following the nonviolent model of Jesus, to create new equitable structures. It means getting our hands dirty and rubbing shoulders with the "other," embodying a gospel mandate to love that puts us right smack in the middle of the mess.

The call to resist evil can be entirely individualized and lead to separatism, or it can include a community perspective that resists evil not only in our personal lives but in our communities. While the premillennial dispensational call is to remain privately holy until the rapture takes us out of the mess, the message of both the prophetic call to reform and the apocalyptic vision of God's new day requires us to engage in the needs of the world and to help usher in the kingdom of God. Unfortunately, this message has been muffled as the volume of premillennial dispensationalism has been turned up by the Left Behind phenomenon.

Confronting the Influence of Premillennial Dispensationalism
LaHaye and Jenkins depict trained theologians as ignorant buffoons who cannot understand their "prophecy teachings." They accuse seminary professors of tricking prospective pastors into believing premillennial dispensational prophecy teachings are not important and conclude that laypeople are far better trained in Bible prophecy than their pastors because they read their books, attend their seminars, and go to their movies.[3] In part, they are correct. Premillennial dispensational understandings are generally not taught in seminary because they are not considered sound interpretations of Scripture, and therefore, many pastors know much less about this view than do their members.

In response to the tragedies of our world and out of a desire for things to be better, many people have developed a fascination with the "end times." Unfortunately, the most accessible sources of information—popular books, television evangelists, and end-time movies—reflect premillennial dispensational teachings, and so this perspective has infiltrated the church. On the other hand, church members receive regular instruction from pastors and educators through sermons and study groups. The result is very mixed-up belief systems that, nonetheless, have taken years to develop and are strongly held. This creates significant problems when pastors are asked questions about recent events and "biblical prophecy," as pastors frequently do not know how to respond. Or if their responses do not involve the quoting of a lot of Scripture texts, parishioners are often unwilling to accept nonpremillennial dispensational understandings as biblical.

I have found in my own congregation and with seminary students that an explanation of the history and theological underpinnings of premillennial dispensationalism opens the door for serious conversation about these teachings. For example, most people firmly believe that God cares equally for everyone. Thus, when confronted by the dispensational notion of an Israel-church dichotomy, they will take pause. Such a moment can open the door for learning, not only about the inherent problems of the theological system behind Left Behind but, more important, for learning more about reading with integrity prophecy, apocalypse, and all the writings of the Bible.

NOTES

CHAPTER 1

1. Tim LaHaye and Jerry B. Jenkins, *Left Behind* (Wheaton, IL: Tyndale, 1995), endorsement page.
2. Tim LaHaye, Jerry B. Jenkins, and Sandi L. Swanson, *The Authorized Left Behind Handbook* (Wheaton, IL: Tyndale, 2005), 33.
3. Tim LaHaye and Jerry B. Jenkins, *Are We Living in the End Times? Current Events Foretold in Scripture . . . and What They Mean* (Wheaton, IL: Tyndale, 1999), x–xi.
4. LaHaye, Jenkins, and Swanson, *Authorized Left Behind Handbook*, 13. A *Time*/CNN poll reports that more than one-third of Americans say they are paying more attention now to how the news might relate to the end of the world. Fifty-nine percent believe the events described in Revelation are going to come true, and nearly one-quarter think the Bible predicted the September 11, 2001 terrorist attacks. Quoted in Timothy P. Weber, *On the Road to Armageddon: How Evangelicals Became Israel's Best Friend* (Grand Rapids: Baker, 2004), 196.
5. LaHaye and Jenkins, *Are We Living in the End Times?* 4–6.
6. LaHaye, Jenkins, and Swanson, *Authorized Left Behind Handbook*, 4.
7. Amy Johnson Frykholm, *Rapture Culture: Left Behind in Evangelical America* (New York: Oxford University Press, 2004), 138.
8. Ibid., 56.
9. LaHaye, Jenkins, and Swanson, *Authorized Left Behind Handbook*, 4.
10. See, e.g., Frykholm, *Rapture Culture*, 53–59.
11. Ibid., 128–29.
12. Jason Byassee, "Enraptured: What's Behind 'Left Behind'?" *Christian Century*, April 20, 2004, 18.
13. Weber, *On the Road to Armageddon*, 14. See also James T. Tabor and Eugene V. Gallagher, *Why Waco? Cults and the Battle for Religious Freedom in America* (Berkeley: University of California Press, 1997).

14. Weber, *On the Road to Armageddon*, 14. See also C. H. Mackintosh, *Papers on the Lord's Coming* (Chicago: Bible Institute Colportage Association, n.d.), 101–2.

CHAPTER 2

1. Justin Martyr and Irenaeus held this view.
2. E.g., Clement of Alexandria, Origen, and Dionysius.
3. Augustine, *The City of God*, book 20, chaps. 3–29. Many have suggested that Augustine was actually an amillennialist.
4. Alexander the Great died in 323 BCE after reigning twelve years, during which time he conquered Greece, Asia Minor, Mesopotamia, Persia, Bactria, and India. Just before his death, Alexander divided his kingdom among his officers. From the time of his death until 175 BCE, when Antiochus Epiphanes IV took control, there was a complex history of power struggles over Alexander's kingdom. The rulers involved in these power struggles are depicted in Daniel 7:7 by the ten horns. The eleventh horn is Antiochus Epiphanes IV. Bruce M. Metzger and Roland E. Murphy, eds., *The New Oxford Annotated Bible* (New York: Oxford University Press, 1994), 1138 Old Testament; 187 Apocrypha.
5. Adolf von Harnack, *What Is Christianity?* (New York: Harper & Row, 1957), 55–56. This is the group that began the now-famous search for the historical Jesus.
6. Albert Schweitzer, *The Quest of the Historical Jesus: A Critical Study of Its Progress from Reimarus to Wrede* (New York: Macmillan, 1964), 395–96.
7. Ibid., 401.
8. C. H. Dodd, *The Apostolic Preaching and Its Developments* (reprint, New York: Harper & Brothers, 1951), 85.
9. J. A. T. Robinson, *Jesus and His Coming: The Emergence of a Doctrine* (New York and Nashville: Abingdon, 1957), 183.
10. Walter Rauschenbusch, *A Theology for the Social Gospel* (1917, reprint Nashville: Abingdon, 1987), 224.
11. Millard Erickson, *Christian Theology* (Grand Rapids: Baker, 1986), 1162–64.

THE FACTS BEHIND THE FICTION

12. In *Christian Zionism: Road-Map to Armageddon?* (Downers Grove, IL: InterVarsity, 2004), 42, 73, Stephen Sizer suggests that Darby is remiss in acknowledging his profound indebtedness to Edward Irving for the "inspiration" of his thought, just as Scofield's reliance on (plagiarism of) Darby was not acknowledged.

13. There is no agreement on the exact number of covenants found in the Bible. However, references are often made to the Edenic, Adamic, Noahic, Abrahamic, Mosaic, Palestinian, Davidic, and new covenants.

14. Paul Boyer, *When Time Shall Be No More: Prophecy Belief in Modern American Culture* (Cambridge: Harvard University Press, 1992), 97; Timothy P. Weber, *On the Road to Armageddon: How Evangelicals Became Israel's Best Friend* (Grand Rapids: Baker, 2004), 39.

15. Albertus Pieters, *A Candid Examination of the Scofield Bible* (Swengel, PA: Bible Truth Depot, 1938), 8.

16. "The Gospel Witness," April 7, 1932, quoted in Pieters, *Candid Examination of the Scofield Bible*, 6.

17. Weber, *On the Road to Armageddon*, 78–79. Paul Boyer, "Apocalypticism in the Modern Age," in Bernard J. McGinn, John J. Collins, and Stephen J. Stein, eds., *The Continuum History of Apocalypticism* (New York: Continuum, 2003), 528.

18. C. C. Ryrie, *Dispensationalism Today* (Chicago: Moody, 1965), 87.

19. The church's relationship to the millennium is not always clear. Some say the church will return at the beginning of the millennium and pass through it to eternal life. Others say they will occupy with Israel a special place in the kingdom. Still others have suggested the church will not return to earth, but will be part of the holy city hovering over the earth. Clarence B. Bass, *Backgrounds to Dispensationalism: Its Historical Genesis and Ecclesiastical Implications* (Grand Rapids: Eerdmans, 1960), 43–44.

20. C. I. Scofield, *The Scofield Reference Bible* (Oxford: Oxford University Press, 1919), 5.

21. Bass, *Backgrounds to Dispensationalism*, 21.

22. Pieters, *Candid Examination of the Scofield Bible*, 10.

CHAPTER 3

1. H.A. Ironside, *Lectures on the Book of Revelation* (New York: Loizeux Brothers, Bible Truth Depot, 1930), 103 quoted in Boyer, 96.
2. H. Richard Niebuhr's famous lecture series (1949), later published in book form, outlines five ways in which the Christian church has understood its relationship to the cultural society in which it exists: Christ Against Culture, Christ of Culture, Christ Above Culture, Christ and Culture in Paradox, Christ the Transformer of Culture. The premillennial dispensational system is clearly located in the first of these five perspectives, Christ against Culture. As such, premillennial dispensationalists strive to draw a clear line between the people of faith and the world. According to this perspective, Christ has come to destroy the works of the devil. Thus the loyalty of the believer is directed solely toward the new order, in this case the end-time events that will be ushered in when Jesus returns. H. Richard Niebuhr, *Christ and Culture* (New York: Harper & Row, 1956).
3. C. I. Scofield, *The Scofield Reference Bible* (Oxford: Oxford University Press, 1919), 1169–70.
4. Timothy P. Weber, *On the Road to Armageddon: How Evangelicals Became Israel's Best Friend* (Grand Rapids: Baker, 2004), 60.
5. Tim LaHaye and Jerry B. Jenkins, *Are We Living in the End Times? Current Events Foretold in Scripture . . . and What They Mean* (Wheaton, IL: Tyndale, 1999), 152–53.
6. The following summary is developed from Ibid., 172–75.
7. Ibid., 172.
8. Ibid., 174.
9. Ibid.
10. Ibid.
11. "Dark Ages," in *Wikipedia*, http://en.wikipedia.org/wiki/Dark-Ages, accessed February 5, 2006. See also European Middle Ages, http://www.wsu.edu:8080/~dee/MA/INTRO.HTM and The Early Middle Ages, http://www.newgenevacenter.org/west/middle.htm
12. The National Huguenot Society, http://www.Huguenot.net nation.com/general/huguenot.htm, accessed February 2006.
13. David L. Edwards, *Christianity: The First Two Thousand Years* (New York: Orbis, 1997), 393.

14. Ernest R. Sandeen, *The Roots of Fundamentalism* (Chicago: University of Chicago Press, 1970), xiv, xix.
15. Council for Secular Humanism, http://www.secularhumanism.org, accessed February 2006.
16. LaHaye and Jenkins, *Are We Living in the End Times?* 132–33, 163, and 172.
17. Ibid., 176–78.
18. See, e.g., Pacific Institute, "Conclusive Proof That the Pope Is the AntiChrist," www.pacinst.co/antichrist.htm; or Ian R. K. Paisley, "The Pope Is the AntiChrist," July 11, 2000, www.ianpaisley.org.
19. LaHaye and Jenkins, *Are We Living in the End Times?* 209–18.

CHAPTER 4

1. David Noel Freedman, et al., eds., "Pre-exilic Hebrew Prophecy," *Anchor Bible Dictionary*, vol. 5 (New York: Doubleday, 1992), 482.
2. The Babylonians took into exile only the leaders of Judah who could/would resist Babylonian dominance. Those left behind were of the lower classes, the uneducated rural population and peasantry. The two groups were separated for nearly fifty years, during which both groups continued their worship of God even though the temple was destroyed. When the exiles returned to Judah and Jerusalem to rebuild the city and the temple, there certainly would have been some tension between these two groups. Paul Hanson, in his book *The Dawn of Apocalyptic*, has suggested the two groups had very different visions for the reconstructed temple. He believes that the group that returned from exile, which he names the Hierocrats, sought to re-create Jerusalem, the temple, and its worship according to their recollection of the golden years of King David. To this group he attributes the writing of Ezekiel, Haggai, Zechariah 1–8, and 1 and 2 Chronicles. In contrast, he believes the second group, which he names the Visionaries, looked for a new supernatural wisdom from above to guide their endeavors. To this group he attributes the beginnings of the biblical apocalyptic literature as evidenced in Isaiah 56–66 and Zechariah 9–14 (Philadelphia: Fortress, 1979, vii–ix). This is one theory on the beginnings of apocalyptic literature; however, there is no agreement

among scholars on how Apocalyptic literature began. Some believe it was born out of the prophetic literature, but others find the two genres too dissimilar to accept the possibility of a dependency. In any event, the scholars do agree that the biblical text does contain the two distinct genres of prophecy and apocalypse.

3. Walter Bauer, et. al., *A Greek-English Lexicon of the New Testament and Other Early Christian Literature*, 2nd ed. (Chicago: University of Chicago Press, 1979), 92.

4. This explanation is drawn from the Society of Biblical Literature Genres project's definition of apocalyptic as "A genre of revelatory literature with a narrative framework, in which a revelation is mediated by an otherworldly being to a human recipient, disclosing a transcendent reality which is both temporal, insofar as it envisages eschatological salvation, and spatial insofar as it involves another, supernatural world. The genre is not constituted by one or more distinctive themes, but by a distinctive combination of elements." Admittedly, this is a complex definition, one that was created and agreed upon by scholars who claim biblical apocalyptic literature as their area of specialization. Nevertheless, it is the definition that will be found in every solid commentary or writing that addresses the apocalypses of the Bible (J. J. Collins, ed., "Apocalypse: Morphology of a Genre," *Semeia* 14, 1979, 9).

5. These nine characteristics are a slightly revised version of Koester's list of important features found in "Apocalypticism in the Hellenistic Era," Helmut Koester, *History, Culture and Religion of the Hellenistic Age: Volume 1: Introduction to the New Testament* (New York: Walter de Gruyter, 1982), 232-233.

CHAPTER 5

1. It was not uncommon for biblical writers to use historical names when referring to contemporary entities. This should be understood as a form of artistry. By using Babylon to refer to Rome, John conjures up memories of the first "world power" to overcome Jerusalem and its temple. Babylon not only conquered Jerusalem, but carried off the elite into exile, where they remained for about fifty years. By addressing Rome as

---

Babylon, the first hearer/reader imposes upon Rome the powerful negative feelings and memories associated with the same, which serves to add fuel to the fire of John's rhetoric. Instead of writing a paragraph or chapter focusing on the evils of Babylon and how the Jews were mistreated by Babylon, and then associating these evils with Rome, he simply calls Rome Babylon. Thus, the association has been made.

2. James C. Vanderkam, *An Introduction to Early Judaism* (Grand Rapids: Eerdmans Pub. Co., 2001), 42-43.

3. The death of Peter and Paul during Nero's persecution is testified to in *The First Epistle to the Corinthians* by Clement of Rome (www.ccel.org/fathers2/ANF-01/anfo1-05.html). While Clement's comments may not be accurate, they provide evidence of rumors about Nero's persecutions. Rumors as well as facts provide the background for the veiled reference to Nero as the Antichrist in Revelation 13:3.

4. The four consecutive world powers were originally Babylon, Media, Persia, and the Greeks. This succession of powers was later reinterpreted to incorporate Rome as the fourth beast: Babylon, Media/Persia, the Greeks, and Rome.

5. "Nero" in David Noel Freedman et al., *The Anchor Bible Dictionary* (New York: Doubleday, 1992), 1076-1081.

CHAPTER 6

1. Tim LaHaye and Jerry B. Jenkins, *Are We Living in the End Times? Current Events Foretold in Scripture . . . and What They Mean* (Wheaton, IL: Tyndale, 1999), 68.

2. Ibid., 78.

3. Ibid., 76–77.

4. Ibid., 69.

5. Ibid., 78.

6. Ibid., 80.

7. Ibid., 81.

8. Tim LaHaye, *The Beginning of the End* (Wheaton, IL: Tyndale, 1972), 65, as quoted in LaHaye and Jenkins, *Are We Living in the End Times?* 86.

Notes

9. LaHaye and Jenkins, *Are We Living in the End Times?* 87.
10. Ibid.
11. Josephus, *Antiquities of the Jews*, 1.123.
12. LaHaye and Jenkins, *Are We Living in the End Times?* 122–29.
13. See, e.g., Revelation 3:12.
14. LaHaye and Jenkins, *Are We Living in the End Times?* 134–38.
15. Ibid., 137. No reference is provided by the authors for where they get this "ancient rabbinic rule."
16. Ibid., 135–36.
17. Ibid., 138–42. Hussein did begin to rebuild Babylon, which is located about fifty-six miles south of Baghdad. However, his building projects, with the exception of his presidential palace, had much the same flavor as today's Disney World, since many of the original Babylonian artifacts have been excavated and are currently housed in foreign museums. All work on the city ceased once Hussein lost control of Iraq. See Stuart Johnson, "Where's Babylon?" http://www.leftbehind.com/channelliveforgod.asp?pageid=708&channelID=159.
18. J. N. Darby, *Reflections upon the Prophetic Inquiry, and the Views Advanced in It*, Col. Writ., Pro. Vol. I, p. 27, as quoted in Clarence Bass, *Backgrounds to Dispensationalism: Its Historical Genesis and Ecclesiastical Implications* (Grand Rapids: Eerdmans, 1960), 129.
19. J.N. Darby, *On the Formation of Churches* in William Kelly, ed., *Collected Writings of J.N. Darby* 32 vols. (London: G. Morrish, 1867–83), 217 as quoted in Bass, *Backgrounds to Dispensationalism*, 105.
20. J. N. Darby, *What Is the Unity of the Church* in William Kelly, ed., *Collected Writings of J.N. Darby* 32 vols. (London: G. Morrish, 1867–83), 455, quoted in Bass, *Backgrounds to Dispensationalism*, 105.
21. The discussion of texts that support the rapture is drawn from Tim LaHaye, Jerry B. Jenkins, and Sandi L. Swanson, *The Authorized Left Behind Handbook* (Wheaton, IL: Tyndale, 2005), 73–81.
22. Ibid., 75.
23. Ibid., numbers 8 and 9. Curly brackets indicate my additions.
24. Ibid., 74.
25. Ibid., 75, numbers 11, 12, and 13. Curly brackets indicate my additions.

26. The Greek word from the phrase "meet the Lord" was a technical expression that referred to a delegation of citizens who would depart the city to meet a dignitary to escort him back into the city. This was intended to give the person the honor and respect due him according to his status and position. The use of this term in this text has been understood by some, including I. Howard Marshall, *1 & 2 Thessalonians*, NCB (Grand Rapids: Eerdmans, 1983), 155, as the depiction of the people of faith meeting Jesus in the air to escort him back to earth where he will reign as King of his kingdom. Marshall is careful, however, not to go beyond what the verse is saying and does not read into it any end-time events. Instead, his focus is on the main point of the text, which is the assuaging of grief.

Abraham J. Malherbe, *The Letters to the Thessalonians*, Anchor Bible (New York: Doubleday, 2000), 277–78, notes that nothing is said about escorting the Lord back to earth, about the group going to heaven, about a bodily transformation, about sharing in the messianic banquet, or about the judgment. He emphasizes that in this context Paul keeps the description of what will occur very lean, focusing only on being with the Lord.

Earl J. Richard, *First and Second Thessalonians*, Sacra Pagina Series, vol. 11 (Collegeville, MN: Liturgical Press, 1995), 247, emphasizes the place of meeting, "in the clouds" and "in the air," as the ethereal region between heaven and earth. As such, he notes that Paul certainly could not have meant they would remain in this region, as it was often associated with demonic activity. Thus he concludes that the group must move either to earth or to the heavens. The group is heavenbound, however, the emphasis in the verse is not on the end times, but on the elect being united with their risen Lord.

Finally, F. F. Bruce, *1 & 2 Thessalonians*, Word Bible Commentary (Waco: Word, 1982), 103, concludes that even though the technical term for escorting a dignitary back into the city appears in this text, there is not enough evidence to determine whether the group will continue on to heaven or return to earth. Similarly, he notes that it is not certain whether the Son of Man coming in the clouds (Daniel 7:13) is headed to earth or back to heaven.

While there is no agreement among scholars on the final destination of the group that gathers in the air, they all acknowledge the unique use of the Greek technical term for escorting a dignitary back into the city. One of the most important interpretive questions here is why Paul would use a technical term instead of everyday language to describe the "meeting" in the air. It seems to me that I. Howard Marshall is right on the money with his interpretation. First Thessalonians is the earliest New Testament writing we have, so reference to later Pauline writings, which are also unclear, as a means of interpreting this verse is iffy. The focus of the verse is on the elect being with the Lord, and nothing more. When a technical term is used in place of an ordinary word commonly found in everyday language, there is a reason; for imposing a theology on the verse, such as the idea that the ultimate goal for the Christian is heaven does not allow the meaning to come from the verse itself.

27. LaHaye and Jenkins are convinced of a premillennial rapture for the church for four reasons. First, they quote Revelation 3:10, which says, "Because you have kept My command to persevere, I also will keep you from the hour of trial which shall come upon the whole world" (NKJV). From this verse LaHaye and Jenkins have concluded that the Lord himself promised to deliver us. The "us" is equal in their minds, due to their premillennial dispensational hermeneutic, to the "true church." Second, God has promised to deliver the church (i.e., the true church) from the wrath to come (1 Thessalonians 1:10). Third, Christians (i.e., true Christians) are not appointed to wrath (1 Thessalonians 5:9). Finally, there is no mention of the church in Revelation 4–18, which is interpreted to mean that the church has already been raptured. (See *The Authorized Handbook*, 73–75.)

28. The Septuagint, the Greek translation of the Hebrew Bible, which LaHaye and Jenkins may be using, could be translated, "And Enoch was well-pleasing to God, and was not found, because God took him up." While this translation has a stronger sense that Enoch may have gone to heaven, it still does not address the idea of a transformed body.

29. LaHaye, Jenkins, *Are We Living in the End Times?* 315–24.

30. See volume twelve of the series, *Glorious Appearing: The End of Days* (Wheaton: Tyndale, 2004), 162–65.

31. LaHaye and Jenkins, and Swanson, 87.

32. LaHaye and Jenkins, *Are We Living in the End Times?* 153.

33. Ibid., 152–53.
34. One would be hard pressed to find a solid commentary on Daniel that disagrees with this interpretation of Daniel 9:24-27. Commentaries that agree that the book of Daniel, including 9:24-27, depicts a summary of historical events from the second century BCE include Robert A. Anderson, *Daniel: Signs and Wonders*, International Theological Commentary (Grand Rapids: Eerdmans, 1984); J. J. Collins, *Daniel*, Hermeneia (Minneapolis: Fortress, 1993); P. R. Davies, "Daniel," *The Oxford Bible Commentary*, ed. John Barton and John Muddiman (Oxford: Oxford University Press, 2001), 568; L. F. Hartman and A. DiLella, *The Book of Daniel*, Anchor Bible, 23 (Garden City, NY: Doubleday, 1978); A. Lacocque, *The Book of Daniel*, trans. D. Pellauer (Atlanta: John Knox, 1979); N. W. Porteous, *Daniel*, 2nd rev. ed. Old Testament Library (London: SCM and Philadelphia: Westminster, 1979); W. S. Towner, *Daniel*, Interpretation: A Bible Commentary for Preaching and Teaching (Atlanta: John Knox, 1984).

CHAPTER 7

1. This outline is a slightly revised version of the outline presented in Tim LaHaye, Jerry B. Jenkins, and Sandi L. Swanson, *The Authorized Left Behind Handbook* (Wheaton, IL: Tyndale, 2005), 62–65. I have added Scripture references where they neglected to include them. The discussion of the characters, events, and story line that follows comes from the *Left Behind* novels and the authors' two nonfiction books *Are We in the End Times?* and *The Authorized Left Behind Handbook*.
2. LaHaye, Jenkins, and Swanson, *Authorized Left Behind Handbook*, 92.
3. Ibid., 27.
4. Tim LaHaye and Jerry B. Jenkins, *Are We Living in the End Times? Current Events Foretold in Scripture . . . and What They Mean* (Wheaton, IL: Tyndale, 1999), 22.
5. Ibid., 226–29.
6. Tim LaHaye and Jerry B. Jenkins, *Glorious Appearing: The End of Days* (Wheaton, IL: Tyndale, 2004), 346–49 (paperback edition).

7. Ibid., 376.

8. LaHaye and Jenkins, *Are We Living in the End Times?* 277.

9. LaHaye, Jenkins, and Swanson, *Authorized Left Behind Handbook*, 86.

10. Ibid.

11. LaHaye and Jenkins, *Are We Living in the End Times?* 365.

CHAPTER 8

1. Also written in response to the crisis imposed upon the Jews during the time of Antiochus Epiphanes IV are Sibylline Oracle #3 (163–145 BCE), 1 and 2 Maccabees (100–63 BCE), and the Animal Apocalypse (165–161 BCE). Over two hundred years later, in response to the crisis of the destruction of the second temple in 70 CE, several more apocalypses were written. Among these writings are the books of Revelation, 4 Ezra (ca. 100 CE), 2 Baruch (ca. 100 CE), and Sybilline Oracle #5 (80–132 CE).

2. *5 Compelling Signs of the End Times,* http://secure.agora-media.com/leftbehind/2004.asp, December 23, 2005.

3. Tim LaHaye and Jerry B. Jenkins, *Are We Living in the End Times? Current Events Foretold in Scripture . . . and What They Mean* (Wheaton, IL: Tyndale, 1999), 74–75.